WONDER WHY?

Fascinating Stories, Fun Facts, Questions & Answers About the Mysteries of Science, History, Pop Culture, and Traditions Around the World!

$2+6=8$

I0559507

RIDDLELAND

INTRODUCTION

"Why?"

"Why" is one of the first words that children learn to say. Children are naturally curious about the world around them, and a "why" question can lead to fascinating revelations. In fact, if you have hung around a three–year–old recently, you may have been driven crazy with all the "why" questions the child asks.

We have all been three–year–olds. We have all asked "why" questions. Sadly, society – because they are short on patience, don't know the answer, or simply want to create robots – have replied "Don't ask why. Just do as I say" and "Just study for the test," and, after a while, many of us have stopped questioning the world around us. We have lost our curiosity and our creativity, and we are preparing for a life as a drone in an office or on an assembly line. Rather than just being another drone, don't you think that it's time to begin asking "why" again?

Some people enjoy being robots, being told exactly what to do, when to do it, and precisely what to think. They don't want to have to make decisions or think for themselves. They are content with believing everything that they see and hear, as long as it meshes with what they already perceive to be true. They are happy with following fads others have started, with buying whatever brand advertises in front of them, and voting for politicians based on rumor instead of fact. If you want more to life than merely work – watch television–sleep–and–repeat, and you do not want to become a helpless, manipulated pawn, you must learn to think for yourself. You must become a critical thinker, a person who constantly asks, "Why?"

Sometimes people mistakenly think that "critical thinking" means thinking negatively about things. Afterall, restaurant critics, movie critics, and opera critics often write very negative articles. However, a critic is someone who can tell good things from bad things; a film critic, for example, can tell a good film from a bad film and can explain both the good qualities and the bad qualities of the film. Similarly, a critical thinker can tell good thinking from bad thinking.

One of the keys to being a critical thinker is to ask "why". Rather than just doing something because someone tells you to – and people are constantly telling us to buy this brand of sneaker or to support this political candidate, the critical thinker will ask "why should I do that?"

Instead of just accepting the world as it is, become a critical thinker and ponder why it is the way that it is. Asking why something is the way that it is currently is the start of realizing that there are alternatives to the status quo; perhaps something can be changed to make the situation even better than it currently is.

Asking "why" questions will not only improve your thinking skills, but it will also improve your language, your knowledge of history and biology, and your communication skills. As you read this book, you will find that not only will your horizons expand, but so will your vocabulary. Also, you will begin to construct interesting why questions of your own. "Why" questions often stimulate one's curiosity. Also, they focus one's attention on a specific issue so that one can find the answer. For instance, "I wonder why my body is the way that it is?" is vague, asking the more specific question of "Why are all of my fingers different lengths?" will lead to an answer. (In fact, that is one of the questions answered within this book.)

Having found the answer to the "why" question, you will feel more self-confident and have more self-esteem. You will be justified in this feeling, for you will indeed be more knowledgeable, will have developed language skills, and will likely have stimulated an interest in learning about the world around you. When you finish this book, you will not only know the answers to the fifty questions in this book, but you will have laid the foundation for life-long learning – you will have good reason to feel good about yourself.

You can read this book cover to cover. If you have a particular interest or are intrigued by a particular question, you can skip directly to it; you don't have to read the sections in any order. Also, this book is a handy reference, and the questions are great conversation starters. It is a book you will likely refer to again and again.

Most of the questions have very specific answers. However, some of the events being questioned happened so long ago, no one is sure of the answer. and, in other cases, science has not reached a conclusive answer. For each article, references are given to prove that the article has been researched and that what is offered in this book is not unfounded. The references also provide a way to learn more about the subject.

In summary, this is a wonderful book that is put together well. The time you spend reading it is time well invested. Now, without further ado, let's get underway.

TABLE OF CONTENTS

PART 1
INTERNATIONAL CUSTOMS

WHY DO THEY RUN THE BULLS IN SPAIN?

Stampede!

Do you think you could outrun a charging herd of angry bulls and steers? The average human can run 5.9 miles (9.5 kilometers) per hour; the average bull can run 15-20 miles per hour (21.4 – 32.2 kilometers). To put it simply, a bull – even though it typically weighs between 1,100 and 2,200 pounds (498 – 997 kgs) pounds - can likely outrun you. Therefore, let's say that you have to run 900 yards (822.96 meters)– that is nine NFL (National Football League) football fields placed side by side and you have to do it in less than two minutes; if you don't, you are going to get trampled. Are you up for the challenge?

Lots of people are! Each year in Pamplona, Spain, literally thousands of people try to outrun the bulls as part of the Sanfermin Festival – known better outside of Spain as the

San Fermin Festival or simply The Running of the Bulls, a festival that honors the regions patron saint with music, running bulls, sangria, and bullfighting. The festival begins with fireworks on the evening of July 6; the next morning marks the highlight of the festival, the Running of the Bulls. If you don't get your courage worked up to try to outrun the stampede on July 7, don't panic – you don't have to wait until next year; a Running of the Bulls will take place each day until the festival concludes on July 14.

Yes, people do get injured doing this. Most slow runners can jump out of the way of the stampeding herd, but should you fall, it is best to just lie there and be trampled; trying to rise to your feet will likely lead to being gored, a fate much worse than being trampled. If you decide to run with the bulls, the safest place to run is in the center of the road; it's sad to say, but people may try to trip you if you run too close to the side.

To keep the bulls from straying downtown or into a residential neighborhood, the route from the bulls' pen to the bullfighting auditorium is outlined with barriers. Should the bulls get close to one of today's runners, the runner, called a mozo, can try to climb up and over one of these barricades. The barricades also provide a place where people can sit and watch the bulls run, and, should someone feel ambitious, one can jump on a bull's back and try to go for a ride.

The Running of the Bulls typically takes about two and a half minutes from the starting gun (literally a firework) being fired in the stockyard to the bulls reaching the auditorium where they will fight matadors later in the day. Two and a half minutes may be typical; however, sometimes the bulls walk part of the course rather than run, and the Running of the Bulls has been known to last over thirty minutes.

The Running of the Bulls has taken place since around the beginning of the second century, evolving from a cattle drive into the production it is today. Around 1100, the bulls to be used in the arena for bullfighting for the newly declared festival of St. Fermin were raised outside of town, and it was necessary to transport the bulls several miles from their farm to the arena. Having the bulls walk as part of a cattle drive was the most efficient means of moving them. People were fascinated with this annual cattle drive and began to come out to see it. Sometimes a showoff would lower himself from a rocky ledge onto a bull's back, and should he fall off, he would have to face the oncoming herd. Eventually, facing the oncoming herd and trying to outrun it became an adrenaline rush people sought – and continue to seek to this day.

FUN FACTS

The use of concrete barriers is a recent addition; in the past, humans lined the path and kept the bulls from stampeding off the course.

The festival began in October in the Middle Ages around 1100 to honor the patron saint of the region, Fermin. Although the festival retains its name, it has lost its religious overtones and has even moved from October to July because the weather in northern Spain is much better for outdoor parties at that time.

In 1926, Ernest Hemmingway described the festival in detail in The *Sun Also Rises*; the popularity of the book caused the festival to become a tourist destination for many people.

Bulls are not the only cattle running at The Running of the Bulls; steers are also part of the mob. Female cattle, though, are not.

No helmets, armor, or protective pads are allowed; neither is going nude. Costumes are banned as well; all runners simply wear their street clothes.

Throughout history, numerous terrorist plots have been attempted to create panic and/or overthrow a government. For instance, in the United States on September 11, 2001, airplanes were hijacked and used as missiles, successfully attacking the economic icon of the nation, the World Trade Center and attempting to fly into the political icons, the capitol/ White House. Citizens on the plane rose up and overcame the terrorists, thwarting the plot, saving the lives of the nation's leaders, and keeping the chaos to a minimum.

Other nations too have had their share of terrorists who have attempted to change the economic and political order. One of the most famous of these attacks was led by Robert Catesby on November 5, 1605, in London, England. Robert's team of terrorists planned to put gunpowder under the parliament building, and then blow up the building with King James I and the country's leaders inside it. Their goal was to create chaos and then install their choice of king.

The group recruited Guy Fawkes, a disgruntled soldier, one of the nation's foremost explosives experts. He willingly agreed to the plan and set about implementing it. Somebody aware of the plot developed a conscience, though, and on October 26 an anonymous letter was sent to the authorities. (To this day, no one knows if the sender was a participant, a spouse or family member, or a priest that somebody confessed to.) The authorities believed what they read, and on November 4, when the authorities conducted a tedious search of the Parliament building, they found Guy Fawkes in the House of Lords guarding 32 kegs of gunpowder, more than enough to accomplish the mission. Word quickly spread that Guy had been caught, and the other members of the gang wasted no time trying to escape; however, none of the thirteen plotters got away; five were killed in a shootout with the sheriff, and eight were arrested and later hanged.

Each year, the citizens of the United Kingdom and some commonwealth countries remember this devious plot on Guy Fawkes Night, also called Guy Fawkes Day, Fireworks Night, Plot Night, and Bonfire Night, November 5, and give thanks that it failed. The first Guy Fawkes Night was the day after Guy's arrest, November 5, 1605; it was a time of celebrating that the nation had survived the rebels' scheme. The celebration included – and still includes - parades, parties, fireworks, and bonfires. As part of the parades, straw effigies called "Guys" – scarecrows meant to represent Guy Fawkes – are carried through the street during the day; these scarecrows are tossed into the bonfires that evening to symbolize people's hatred for the plot. The fireworks are meant to remind people of the gunpowder that never exploded on the day of the intended assassination. Another custom associated with Guy Fawkes Night is to search the Parliament building for copycats; this ritual was likely started as something very serious but has now, over 500 years later, become light-hearted.

Because all the plotters were Roman Catholics and King James was a Protestant, in generations past Guy Fawkes Night was a time when anti-Catholic prejudice surfaced. As noted in the above essay, today's generation doesn't care what religion the terrorists were; the fact that they were terrorists is reason enough to villainize them.

Guy Fawkes was one of eight of the terrorists who stood trial; all eight were found guilty.

The term "guy" referred to the face of the masks made to look like Guy that were worn at the festival, and children would tease someone who looked like the mask, calling him a "guy". Although children in America may not realize it, when they say, "You guys" or "guys" – an expression which can refer to both men and women, they are referencing the Guy Fawkes masks.

The saying that "History is written by the winners" applies here. Although Guy Fawkes was considered a terrorist and citizens were trained to think of him that way, some people perceived him as a hero and a freedom fighter in both his own day and today.

Effigies of Guy Fawkes are not the only effigies to have been put into the bonfire. Every generation has roasted its perceived enemies; effigies of people you may have heard of include the Pope, Russian leader Vladimir Putin, and the British politician Margaret Thatcher.

WHY DO WE SAY "BLESS YOU" WHEN SOMEONE SNEEZES?

People do not sneeze in their sleep.

It's true, and I can say it with complete confidence. The purpose of a sneeze is to clear the mucus and the airways of foreign particles like mold, dust, and pollen; and, just as we switch off lights in our homes before we go to bed, the brain switches off the nerves that trigger sneezing before we go into a deep sleep. Now, here is something that I can say with only slightly less confidence – if you are in the United States, Great Britain, or any other English-speaking nation and you sneeze, someone around you is going to say, "Bless you."

"Bless you" is short for "God bless you," which is also sometimes said. How this custom came to be is up for debate. According to legend, Pope Gregory I insisted in 590 C.E. that upon hearing someone sneeze, everyone was to pray for he person; medical science had concluded that the sneeze was the first sign that the individual had a touch of the Black Death, a plague that was sweeping the civilized world, and therefore everyone needed to petition God on the person's behalf for good health.

Because most people who had the Bubonic Plague didn't get well, the "bless you" also came to mean "good luck" and "God be with you" on one's journey to Eternal Life. Regardless of whether the sneezer was going to need the blessing to get well or to travel to the Next World, the sneezer definitely needed a blessing.

Other reasons for pronouncing God's blessing upon the sneezer also existed. Some people believed the sneeze was the body's way of exorcizing a demon; others believed that breathing in from a sneeze was the perfect chance for a demon to enter the body – whether the demon was coming or going, the person needed a blessing to be protected from the demon. Other people thought the soul itself – the life within the body - could be expelled from the body with a sneeze, and that it was only by the grace of God that the soul returned to the body.

Where some people perceived the body dying from lack of a soul, others believed that sneezing caused the heart to stop. A quick prayer of, "God bless you," was thought to restart the heart and save the sneezer's life.

By 750 C.E., saying "bless you" after a sneeze had become customary, and many people said it without knowing the reason behind why they said it. Today, saying, "Bless you," after a sneeze is as automatic as saying, "You're welcome" after somebody says "Thank you;" regardless of whether you really mean what you say, social manners call for saying it.

FUN FACTS

"Gesundheit," is the second most common phrase people use when someone sneezes in the United States and the most common phrase said in Germany; it is the German word for "health".

One's heart doesn't stop when one sneezes, but one's heartbeat can be affected by the sneeze.

A single sneeze can release 100,000 germs.

The gusts of air that occur with a sneeze can reach 100 miles-per-hour.

People always close their eyes to sneeze.

Before we begin our discussion, let's remember to be respectful. Let's not call what they wear "skirts"; let's call them "kilts" just as the Scottish do. If you are the typical U.S. male, you are likely arguing that they are skirts and therefore they should be called that. If that is the case, though, why don't we call your "action figures" such as your twelve-inch G.I. Joe and your Batman figurine, "dolls". In general, in many places in the United States it is a cultural taboo for a boy to play with "dolls", but a boy is more than encouraged to play with action figures. So, yes, I know they are "skirts" and you know they are "skirts", but if the term "skirts" is being used derogatorily to suggest that they lack manhood, we should avoid it.

The kilt was invented in Scotland around 1500. It was a full-length garment that slipped over the head or wrapped around the shoulder and then draped around the body to slightly below the knees. The kilt caught on quickly in Scotland because of two practical reasons. One, the kilt kept the wearer warm and dry in the cold and damp Scottish Highland. Two, the Scots found the kilt to be a lot more comfortable than pants, allowing for much greater movement. Most early kilts had a tartan pattern on them and were made of wool – sheep were abundant in the Scottish Highlands. Kilt-wearing quickly spread to other peoples, including the English, Welsh, Cornish, and Irish.

The full-body kilt may have been first, but it is not the most popular kilt today. Around 1700, the "small kilt" or "modern kilt" became fashionable. Whereas the "great kilt" covered the entire body, the small kilt only covered from the waist to the knees. Just like the great kilt, though, these were woolen with a tartan pattern. If you look closely, though, you will notice that the pattern of the tartan varies; this is because different families have different family traditions. Meanwhile, to separate themselves from the Scottish, the Irish often wear a single colored kilt.

The kilt has come to symbolize Scottish culture, and since tartans celebrate one's family heritage, wearing a kilt is something Scottish men – and women – do with pride. The kilt isn't just worn in Scotland, though. In fact, if you are a heavy sweater, don't be surprised if one day your doctor suggests you wear a kilt too, because kilts allow the body's skin to breathe easier than jeans or trousers do. Whereas most fashion trends come and go, 500 years may have passed, but the kilt continues to remain popular in Scotland and elsewhere.

FUN FACTS

The great kilt was the only garment the Scottish Highlanders wore. T-shirts, dress shirts, and similar garments are worn with the small kilt.

The original kilts were very plain, containing no buttons, pockets, belt loops, zippers, studs, or buckles.

Most people wearing kilts do not wear underwear.

The great tartan was used as a blanket as well as an outfit.

Until 1792, if you wanted to wear a kilt in England, you had to join the army. The British believed the freedom of movement the kilt allowed put its soldiers in danger from any citizen that wore it.

Have you ever played the game "Telephone"; the game also goes by the names "Gossip" and "Grapevine". Telephone is a large-group game with the objective of getting a message word-for-word person-by-person from the person who presents it to the last person in the line. The end result is usually very different from the beginning, for people paraphrase the message, edit the message, and sometimes even deliberately sabotage the message. If you can imagine what happens in a game of Telephone, you can understand why Germans call The Easter Bunny "The Easter Hare".

Hares and bunnies are two similar but very different animals. Similarities include long ears, fuzzy tails, fluffy bodies, and strong legs. Although they look similar, hares are generally bigger and stronger, and they have longer ears. Hares tend to live isolated lives – living by themselves or with a partner, but bunnies prefer living around twenty-or-so other bunnies. Hares tend to sleep during the day while bunnies sleep at night. Their diets and temperaments are different as well; hares are not domesticated and like to eat bark and plant stems; bunnies can be tamed into pets and like to eat soft plants and leaves.

If you look at pictures of the critter that delivers the Easter eggs to American children today, you can tell that it is indeed a bunny. However, if you go back to the first book scholars have found mentioning the egg-carrying critter, he was a hare. He was first described in a book for Germans in 1692 and was very well known throughout Germany at that time. In that book, he had a lot of traits of Santa, including determining if boys and girls were naughty and nice and carrying toys for kids as well as eggs and candy.

When the Germans migrated to the United States, the legend of the Easter Hare came with them. However, hares were not as plentiful in North America as bunnies, and so it wasn't long before children began to picture him as a bunny. People became confused because in North America the jackrabbit is actually a hare while the term "rabbit" is used to refer to a bunny. Because of the jackrabbit's name, over the years the "Easter Hare" became the "Easter Rabbit" and then became the "Easter Bunny".

Both Christians and pagans saw symbolism in both the hare and the egg, and atheists saw good, clean fun. Eggs and hares were symbols of fertility in the pagan world, and they were an important part of spring festivals designed to bless the crops. Meanwhile, Christians perceived the hare, which seemed to reproduce magically, as a reminder that Mary was a virgin. Meanwhile, as early as the first century, the Church used the symbol of a chick coming from a "dead" egg to symbolize the Resurrected Christ coming out of the tomb. The Easter Bunny was welcomed by all – as He is today.

FUN FACTS

The United States has three hares: the snowshoe hare, the black-tailed jackrabbit, and the white-tailed jackrabbit. There are 40 species of hares around the world.

A rabbit's teeth grow its entire life.

A "rabbit" and a "bunny" are the same thing; a "rabbit" is the more scientific term. In the past a "bunny" was a term of endearment given to women – bunnies are cute, cuddly, and soft. (Be careful if you call someone a "bunny" today, though; a lot of women will take offense to it.)

Due to disease and predators, typical bunnies in the wild live two years; a pet bunny, though, typically lives eight years and can live up to twelve years.

The German word for the Easter Hare is "Osterhase".

I have a confession to make. When I first heard of Boxing Day, I thought it was a day in which people gathered to watch two people step into a boxing ring and beat each other until one was knocked out. I was appalled that such a brutal sport would be celebrated during the season of "love, joy, and peace on earth". If you thought of the same thing, you'll be relieved to know that Boxing Day has nothing to do with the so-called sport of boxing.

Boxing Day occurs on December 26, the day after Christmas, and "boxing" refers to literally filling boxes. This holiday has roots in the British aristocracy of the Middle Ages, and it is still celebrated in the United Kingdom and many countries which used to be a part of the British Commonwealth. On Christmas Day in the Middle Ages, servants were expected to stay where they worked and serve the lords, ladies, and children of the household. On December 26, though, these servants were excused from working and were encouraged to go be with their families for a Christmas celebration. These servants often received boxes of food to take with them and/or gift-wrapped boxes with items of appreciation of the servant's hard work throughout the year.

Boxing Day was also a day to think of those less fortunate. Lower-class people might not have had servants, but they shared the spirit of giving with people of less fortune, reaching out to the poor and homeless. December 26 had been the Feast of St. Stephen since the Early Church; December 26 was the second day of Christmas in the traditional Twelve Days of Christmas, and giving alms to the poor on that day was already a firm tradition by the Middle Ages.

As British society has changed, so has Boxing Day. Although few people have servants today, Boxing Day remains a popular holiday. In fact, since most people are on the five-day work week, should December 26 fall on a Saturday, the following Monday will be given as a holiday. Although it is still a time in which people think of the poor and try to meet their needs, in recent times, Boxing Day has become a major shopping day, with people freely spending the Christmas cash and gift cards they have been given, and a day for watching premier soccer matches.

FUN FACTS

Whereas English-influenced areas celebrate Boxing Day on December 26, most of the rest of Europe celebrates the Feast of St. Stephen or The Second Day of Christmas. In England or elsewhere, you are not likely to have to report to work on December 25 or 26.

Boxing Day boxes are becoming replaced with bonuses. Whereas delivery people, such as those who bring milk, the newspaper, and the mail used to get a gift box, today they are more likely to receive cash in an envelope.

Because Boxing Day has become a day in which people focus on shopping and watching soccer, most people give their "boxes" to the delivery personnel in early December rather than wait until December 26.

If someone enjoyed too much merriment on Christmas Day, that person can use Boxing Day as a day to recover.

If you are invited to someone's house for a meal on Boxing Day, you will likely be eating Christmas leftovers.

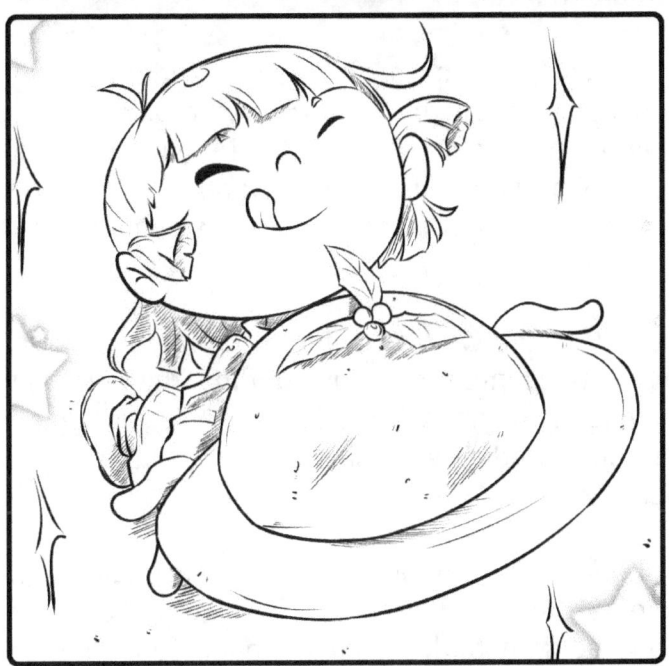

Here in the United States, we tend to thaw our frozen turkeys a couple of days before Thanksgiving Day. Seeing that turkey can make your mouth water! A couple of days seems like an eternity. Can you imagine waiting five weeks for something to cook? If you want good figgy pudding though, that's how long it takes to make – five weeks. Therefore, if you want figgy pudding on Christmas Day, you need to mix all the ingredients together five weeks before Christmas, douse them with brandy, and let them sit in a cool dry place until Christmas.

Figgy pudding originated in the United Kingdom in the Middle Ages and is still popular there and in much of Europe. In the United States, we sing about it, although most people don't know what it is. For instance, in the song *We Wish You A Merry Christmas* the second verse declares, "Now bring us some figgy pudding" and the third verse states, "For we all like figgy pudding." (See the list of references in the back of the book if your mind is suddenly drawing a blank about the words to this traditional carol.)

If you're picturing a custard-like pudding like you will receive in restaurants in the United States if you order "pudding", you're picturing it wrong; in the United Kingdom, "pudding" is a term used to encompass a wide variety of desserts. Figgy pudding certainly isn't custardy; it is a steamed cake, a fruit cake to be more exact.

Don't let the word "fig" fool you either. Although some may have put figs into their figgy pudding, the term fig in Great Britain refers to "raisins". The original recipe for figgy pudding had thirteen ingredients; raisins and currants were the most prominent.

Although figgy pudding can be eaten at any time, it is considered a Christmas Day dish. On Christmas Day, the cook will steam the figgy pudding for 1 ½ hours, put a sprig of holly on top, bring the dessert to the table, douse it with brandy, and then light it on fire. Once the fire is out, the happy revelers can feast on the cake.

Figgy pudding is rich in symbolism. The thirteen ingredients are to remind Christians of Jesus and the twelve disciples. The sprig of holly placed on top is a reminder of the crown of thorns Jesus wore during The Passion and the bright light created by the burning brandy is a reminder of The Resurrection and Glory of Christ. For most Christians, Christmas would have been just another birth – although a miraculous birth, if Jesus had not risen from the grave, and figgy pudding reminds Christians of the Easter story while they are still celebrating the Christmas story.

Figgy pudding ideally ages five weeks; however, if you procrastinate until Christmas Eve, it is still possible to have a figgy pudding Christmas Day. Figgy pudding can be assembled in 30 minutes and cooked for eight hours.

A Christmas Carol, the Charles Dickens classic novel in which Ebeneezer Scrooge encounters the ghosts of Christmas Past, Present, and Future, mentions figgy pudding.

The ingredients in figgy pudding depend on one's tastes. Typical ingredients are cherries, cranberries, currants, oranges, plums, and raisins, and spices such as cinnamon, cloves, ginger, and nutmeg.

Whereas door-to-door Christmas caroling had originated to spread the gospel story in the 1200s, enterprising lower-class members of society went door to door spreading holiday cheer hoping to receive holiday treats like figgy pudding in return.

We Wish You a Merry Christmas was first sung in the late 1500s.

WHY DO PEOPLE HIT PINATAS?

Have you ever heard the slogan, "If you can't beat them, join them?" If you've heard it and want to see it applied, look no further than the pinata.

Although Western culture generally assumes that the pinata originated in Mexico, it was really developed independently first in China, then Mexico, and then Europe. That's right, when the Spanish landed in central and south America, Spain already had the pinata in its culture.

The world's first pinata was likely an ox-shaped vase stuffed with seeds; it was used as part of the Chinese New Year's celebration around 1200. The Chinese would hit the pinata with bags of seeds, causing the pinata to break as a way of ushering in the Chinese New Year. The fact that the Chinese had pinatas was not known by the rest of the world, so the modern pinata used in Western culture has no ties to these early pinatas.

The tradition of the pinata was developed later independently by the Aztec nation in Mexico, Central America, and South America as a way of celebrating the birthday of Huitzilopochtli, the Aztec god of war and fire. In mid-December of each year, the Aztecs would put the pinata, a colorful clay pot that had been decorated with feathers, above the altar dedicated to Huitzilopochtli and then hit it with a stick, releasing a gift on the altar to Huitzilopochtli. Although the pinata had never really caught on in Asia where it originated, in the central and southern parts of the New World, it was deeply embedded in the culture.

Just as the Asians and South Americans had independently invented the pinata, so had the Europeans. As you might suspect, when the Christian missionaries saw the people worshiping Huitzilopochtli with the pinata, they were not happy – they wanted people to worship Yahweh. Their first reaction was to ban all pinata use, but the Aztecs would have none of that.

Here is where the "if you can't beat them, join them" comes in – rather than ban pinatas, the missionaries suggested that they become a part of Christianity. Since around 336 C.E., Christians had been celebrating the birthday of Jesus on December 25. Since Huitzilopochtli's birthday fell in mid-December, the priests decided that the natives could still have their annual birthday party and still have their annual pinata; they just needed to make a couple of changes. One, they needed to celebrate the birth of Jesus and not mention Huitzilopochtli. Two, rather than have an offering to Huitzilopochtli fall out of the pinata, the pinata was to be filled with candy.

The missionaries also used the revamped pinata as a teaching tool. They explained how evil was to be fought, just like one took the stick to hit the pinata. They also explained that if you defeated evil, then you received a reward, just as when the pinata was defeated it would release its toys and candy.

Gradually, the generations that knew the pinata as a tool for worshiping Huitzilopochtli were replaced by a generation that had only heard of it associated with Yahweh.

Today, the pinata is still used at Christmas festivals and other special events. Although the rules of how to strike the pinata vary – typically someone is blindfolded, spun around, and then allowed one swing; if they are unsuccessful, the blindfold is passed to the next person. Although more pinatas sell around Christmas than at any other time of the year, the religious connotations have been removed from it. Most pinata parties don't have priests present to explain the symbolism, so children don't understand why they hit the pinata; they just know that if they hit it just right then will provide candy for everyone – and that's good enough.

FUN FACTS

"Pinata" is from the Italian word meaning "pot"; most early pinatas were clay pots and vases.

The Spanish missionaries generally made a pinata in the shape of a seven-pointed star; each point represented one of the Seven Deadly Sins – lust, gluttony, greed, sloth, anger, pride, and envy.

Today, most pinatas are made from paper mâché.

Pinatas are generally filled with candy and small toys for kids. However, they can be filled with almost anything, and pranksters have used confetti, honey, water, and flour.

In the United States, pinatas are typically filled with candy; in Mexico, they are filled with candy and oranges.

Men wearing white wigs used to be popular in both the United Kingdom and the United States. If you look at pictures of English balls and galas, you will see men wearing them; if you look at pictures of the American Presidents, you'll notice that the early ones almost always have on a wig. Wigs were a symbol of authority and were worn by most leaders; they were also a symbol of being well-to-do, and most upper-class men wore them in public.

Around 1800, the popularity of the wig ran out, and men no longer wore them. If you want to see a man in a white wig there is only one place you are guaranteed to find him – in the British courtroom where a criminal is being tried. Judges, lawyers, and barristers all wear them.

Wig wearing in the court began in the late 1600s. Prior to the official adaptation in 1685, the dress code for a lawyer was to simply keep one's beard and hair neatly trimmed. During the reign of King Charles the II, though, wig wearing became popular in society, and, by the end of his reign, wearing a wig in the courtroom was the norm.

By the time wig-wearing lost its popularity in society, the wig had become such a fixture in the courtroom that law officials kept wearing them. The wig suggested authority; it also showed a continuity with tradition. The judge and lawyers might be just like other people outside of the courtroom, but, once the wig was on, the judge and lawyers were to be revered. Wearing the wig continues to be a reminder to the wearer of an obligation to be impartial and, by hiding the judge's hair color and identity, a reminder to the citizens that justice is blind.

The wigs worn in the courtroom today are slightly different than they were in 1685. Whereas those wigs generally had long sideburns and fell to the back of one's shoulders, today's wigs generally form a bobtail. On formal occasions, though, full-bottomed wigs can still be seen. In general, judges will wear long, curly white wigs and barristers wear shorter, grayer wigs.

Wigs may be losing their popularity among law professionals. As of 2007, a law passed making them non-mandatory for civil and family courts; they are also not required in the Supreme Court. As they have been over 300 years, though, wigs are still required in the British criminal court.

FUN FACTS

Early wigs were made from human hair, but horsehair soon became the norm until just the past few years.

Today, wigs worn in the courtroom are made of horsehair, hemp, or synthetic material.

The wig-wearing fad was popular in England and her colonies; the fad did not originate in England; the fad began in the French courts.

Although judges typically wear black robes, wearing a green, violet, or scarlet robe is acceptable.

An official barrister wig has four rows of seven curls on the back

Oktoberfest in Munich, Germany, is the world's largest annual folk festival. Activities include folk-dancing, enjoying German food and drink, riding carnival rides, and seeing men and women in traditional German dress. Although the Munich festival formally began in 1810, the festival itself has roots going back to the Bavarian culture of the Middle Ages. As you might suspect, with a name like Oktoberfest the festival celebrates autumn, but don't let the name fool you – most of it does not take place in October.

That's right, Oktoberfest is primarily a September festival. It spans 16 to 18 days each year beginning in mid-September and ending the first Sunday of October.

The modern festival began on October 17, 1810; it was designed by government officials to give the common person a chance to celebrate both the recent wedding of Bavaria German prince Ludwig – the future King Louis I - to princess Theresa, and the recent recognition of Bavaria as a German state. The meadow on which it was held in 1810, named Theresienwiese in honor of Theresa, is still the meadow on which the festival is held today. Horse racing, which still takes place, was the primary source of entertainment at the first Oktoberfest.

The citizens enjoyed the festival so much that they wanted it to become an annual tradition; however, the government refused to pay for it. The local Bavarian Agricultural Association agreed to help fund the festival in 1811, but it changed the focus from the wedding of the prince to agriculture. The festival now showed off prize agriculture, much like many U.S. state fairs do today. In 1815, the sponsors changed the course of the festival again – this time unintentionally- when they added beer sales. The festival morphed noticeably again when the City of Munich began sponsorship in 1819, and it has continued to evolve into what it is today.

The original festival had been in mid-October after the harvest season was over, but Munich's city officials soon realized that if they wanted to meet their goals of informing the world about German culture and promoting tourism, they could not keep the date in the rainy, cold October weather. Although the festival had begun as a celebration intended for the local citizens, it had become a great source of revenue for local businesses because of tourists. The city decided to try hosting the festival in mid-September in 1890, and it was such a success that it was permanently placed there in 1905.

Although Oktoberfest is officially celebrated in Munich, you can find Oktoberfests throughout the world. It is a time for Germans to recall and to share their heritage, including good food and beverages, and for all participants to have a good time together.

FUN FACTS

More than six million people attend the Oktoberfest in Munich each year.

At the festival, many Germans wear traditional German costumes; the women wear dresses known as dirndls and the German men wear traditional leather shorts known as lederhosen with an alpine hat.

Over two million gallons of beer are consumed during Oktoberfest each year.

The festival has been canceled 26 times due to pandemics and wars, including World War I and World War II.

Breweries build temporary beer halls on the festival grounds; one beer hall can hold 6,000 people.

If someone were to read you a chapter from this book, would you clap to show your appreciation when they finished?

The answer is yes, you likely would if other people in the room were doing it. On the other hand, if no one else was to do it, you likely would not either. Today, most people clap because they want to fit in with other people.

It hasn't always been that way. Back when civilizations were just getting started and people would gather around the fire to tell stories and sing songs, people would whoop and holler, stomp, and whistle. People made noise if they liked something and wanted it to continue. Whereas riotous stomps might drown out what one wanted to hear, clapping did not. Clapping soon became the most common non-vocal noise made by humans.

By 600 BCE, clapping for something one liked was the social norm. Greek and Roman politicians could tell how popular an idea was based on how loud the applause was. (They could also tell how unpopular it was based on how many rotten tomatoes and other disgusting items were thrown at them.) Audiences were expected to interact with the politicians by both clapping and throwing things. Like politicians, theater actors that did well tended to receive claps, and those who performed poorly were pelted with rotten fruit.

This tradition continued until the 1880s. When Ludwig von Beethoven, Franz Liszt and other classical musicians played, they wanted people to clap throughout the performance; in fact, if there was enough clapping, they would repeat a section of music for the enjoyment of the audience. The social norm changed, though, around the 1880s when classical composer Richard Wagner asked the audience to wait until the end to clap so the piece could be played as a unit without encores. Since then, the social norm is to not interact with classical music during its performance.

Although clapping to show appreciation is a universal gesture, the exact moments to clap are determined by one's culture. In the United States, people are not supposed to clap during classical concerts, but they are expected to at sporting events. Whether at the professional stadium, the local YMCA, or the high school, people will often clap for their favorite sports team when it enters the field, when it pulls off a great play, and when it exits the field; cheerleaders and mascots try to motivate the crowd to keep the noise coming and cue the crowd when to clap. Although society has made some clapping taboo, clapping is still one of the best ways to express one's appreciation and to show agreement with what one is clapping for.

FUN FACTS

In ancient Greece, people were hired by playwrights to clap, encouraging the audience to clap, and thereby raising the approval level of the play; the official job title of the clapper was "claquer".

Just like they clap for sports teams taking the field, people today tend to clap for politicians as they walk onto the stage; the clapping shows appreciation for what the politician has done in the past and/or for the politician's ideas.

A super slow clap is generally a sign of mockery.

The typical person can clap 2.5 to 5 times per second.

Researchers have not found a way to distinguish male claps from female claps; everybody's clap sounds alike.

WHY IS THE PEACE SIGN SHAPED THE WAY IT IS?

The peace symbol is a symbol that is recognized by cultures around the world. Although the peace symbol debuted in London in April 1958, to understand why it looks the way it does, we need to go back to the early 1800s, and, if we want to thank the true inspiration behind it, all the way to the days of the Roman Empire.

Although we take smartphones, the Internet, and the radio for granted, those inventions weren't around until recently. If ships of the Roman navy were to communicate with each other, they couldn't use the radio, so Rome developed a system of semaphore flags. One person would stand at the back of the boat and hold the two flags in different positions to represent different letters. A person in the next boat would see these bright flags and would be able to interpret the message that was being sent.

The Romans may have invented the technology, but it didn't become popular until the 1800s. One of the people who learned it was Gerald Holtom. In February of 1958, Gerald created what eventually became known as "the peace sign" as a symbol for nuclear disarmament. While the United States, United Kingdom, and the Soviet Union – often referred to as Russia, one of the Soviet Union's many members – stockpiled the latest nuclear weapons, people like Gerald wanted all sides to throw away those weapons. He drew a circle, and within that circle he placed a flagger holding a "N" for "nuclear" overlaid on a flagger holding a "D" for "disarmament". Although he had intended to create a symbol for nuclear disarmament and for his group, the Campaign for Nuclear Disarmament, when people saw protestors carrying signs with the symbol at a London protest a couple of months later, they widened the meaning to be no war in general, not just no to nuclear weapons.

Although Holtom invented the peace symbol based on semaphore letters, it was later discovered that his symbol was not unique. The same three-pronged, long-stemmed design had been used in cultures of the past. Whereas Holtom saw semaphore flags, other people saw a crow's foot or an upside-down broken cross. In past generations, the crow's foot had been a symbol of impending death; it was a bad omen. Likewise, the Christian Church had speculated that Satan worshipers held the upside-down broken cross in high reverence. Symbols are constantly changing in meaning though, and most people readily accepted Holtom's explanation, and the symbol took on a new meaning for the new generation.

People had come from around the world to be a part of the London peace march. People such as Bayard Rustin were so impressed with the peace symbol that they shared it with their friends in their native lands. Bayard Rustin, one of the protesters, happened to be a friend of Martin Luther King, Jr., and is credited with bringing the symbol to the United States. Needless to say, with all of this publicity, the peace symbol began to appear in rallies and marches around the world – and it still does.

FUN FACTS

The peace symbol is not copyrighted; you are free to use it any way that you want.

The word "semaphore" is Greek; it literally means "sign bearer".

The peace sign contains the semaphoric letters "N" and "D" for nuclear disarmament. The D is the vertical line in the center of the peace sign and the "N" is the downward lines on either side of the vertical line.

Holtom liked the design not only because it contained the "N" and "D" for nuclear disarmament, but he also liked it because he thought it looked like a person with their hands to their side questioning.

Some American soldiers in Vietnam wore the peace symbol on their helmet to symbolize their displeasure with the war.

What would you think if I were to take 9,999 blue marbles and one red marble, mix them together in a giant canister, blind myself, and then reach into the canister and pull out the red marble?

You'd likely think that I was pretty lucky. Well, the odds of finding a four-leaf clover in a field of clover is 1 to 10,000. Needless to say, the person who found the four-leaf clover had just proven to be very lucky.

The four-leaf clover not only showed to the world who was lucky, it also provided luck as well. Children of the Middle Ages believed that the holder could see fairies. What had become a child's game in the Middle Ages had a much more serious tone with the Ancient Celtics, who believed that the person wearing the four-leaf clover was able to see evil spirits approaching and therefore had time to escape.

A four-leaf clover is a deformed version of the three-leaf clover. As the white clover plant, trifolium repens, seeks to retain its spot in the world, it produces some abnormalities as well as lots of traditional offspring. In evolution, abnormalities tend to die out, but, in some cases, the abnormality becomes the new norm. Three and four-leaf clovers are the most common forms of the plant, but it can grow up to 56 leaves. Four leaf clovers are rare, one out of 10,000, but those odds make it reasonable that you will see one somewhere during your lifetime. The odds of seeing a 56-leaf clover are so high, though, that very few people get to experience it except in pictures.

Have you ever heard the phrase, "The luck of the Irish?" The phrase is rooted in how plentiful the four-leaf clover is in Ireland. Ireland has lush green meadows of clover, and even though the odds are still about 1 in 10,000, there are lots of four-leaf clovers to be found. If you do find a four-leaf clover, look around for others; if the parent plant's genetics have the chromosome that causes four-leaf clovers, the trait will likely show up in several of its offspring.

FUN FACTS

Although some people use the term "shamrock" to describe both a three-leaf clover and a four-leaf clover, by definition, a shamrock is a three-leaf clover.

Beware of frauds. The oxalis deppei plant has four leaves and is often mistaken for clover.

The only 56-leaf clover ever known was found in Japan in 2009.

The shamrock has become associated with St. Patrick and each of its leaves represent a piece of the Trinity – Father, Son, and Holy Spirit. The four-leaf clover also has had meaning assigned to its leaves by society but not the Church – faith, hope, luck, and love.

Most people are lucky to find one four-leaf clover; one person has 160,000 of them!

Ever since the dawn of time, people have been fascinated in how they look. The earliest people could see their reflections in the stagnant water of ponds and puddles. They didn't understand the physics of how light was reflecting off of the water to show what was in front of it; many believed that not only was one's physical image cast into the water, so was one's soul. Hence, if a ripple were to cross the water, people would assume that a ripple was going to come into their life.

The earliest mirrors were flat rocks that would reflect people's image. These may have been found by chance, but by 6000 BCE people were manufacturing them. When metalworking came about around 4000 BCE, bronze mirrors became commonplace. By the Roman Empire, people had learned to coat the mirror with silver for less blurriness. Glass mirrors emerged around 100 BCE.

Glass provided a much clearer image of oneself than previous materials; unfortunately, glass mirrors were prone to breaking. People still believed that the mirror captured one's image and held it. They also believed that the eyes were the gateway to the soul, and that the mirror was capable of holding one's image until it locked into someone else's image. Therefore, if you were the last thing that the mirror saw before it broke, your soul was trapped inside the mirror. People believed that it took seven years for a soul to heal, and therefore you were going to be without a full soul for the coming seven years. Talk about unlucky! That's why people began to say, "If you break a mirror, you will have seven years of bad luck." (Remedies for avoiding bad luck were available, though. For instance, if you put all of the pieces of the broken mirror into a fabric bag or a paper sack, then by reuniting all of the pieces the soul could return to its owner.)

Primitive people thought a ripple in pond water was the foretelling of bad luck; just as the image in the pond water was thought to be predictive of one's future, the image in the mirror was too. Mirrors began to be attributed with magical powers, such as the power to foretell the future. They were also thought to store memories of all they had seen, just as your brain can remember what it has seen. Although different cultures have different customs and beliefs about breaking mirrors, in almost all cultures the break of the mirror is bad luck.

Why did parents so readily pass on the superstition to their children? The truth is that mirrors used to be very expensive, and so parents did not want their children to break them. Telling the tale that breaking a mirror would cause severe misery was a way that parents kept their gullible children in line. By the time the child realized the mirror held no magical qualities, the child was ready to start a family of one's own.

FUN FACTS

Humans do not recognize their own reflections in a mirror until they are about 18-months old.

Many cultures believe that mirrors reflect the soul. Hence, they believe that demons, vampires, and other soul-less creatures cannot see themselves in a mirror.

During the Victorian era, mirrors were always covered when a dead body was present because of fear that the dead person's soul might get caught in the mirror.

If you hold writing to a mirror, it will appear backwards.

In some places, the dead are buried with a mirror in their casket; the mirror is to make sure the soul does not escape.

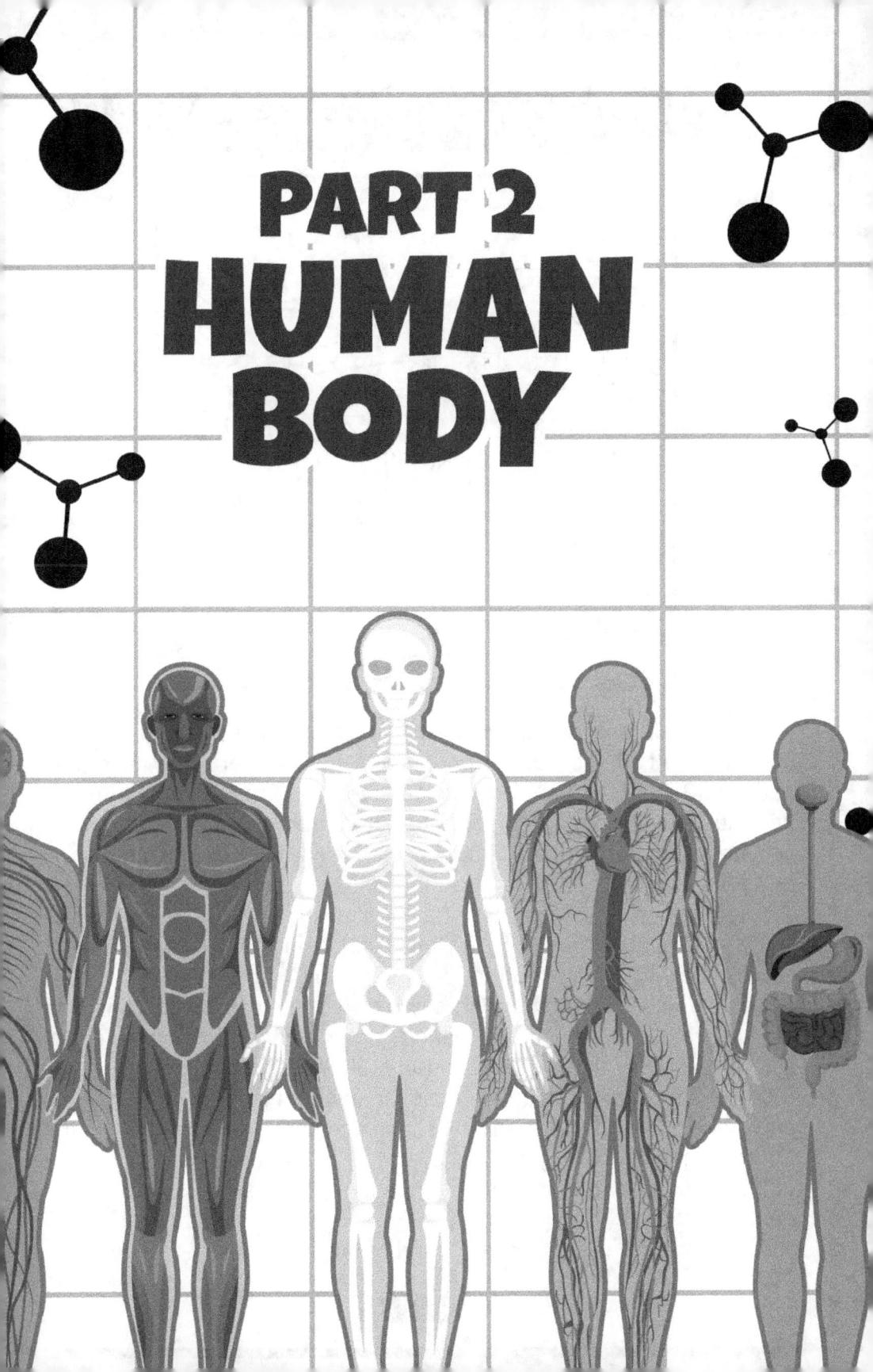

PART 2
HUMAN BODY

WHY DO MOST PEOPLE SNORE WHEN SLEEPING?

Do you snore? Almost everyone snores at some time in their life; over half of the human population snores every now and then, and over 25% of the population snore every time they sleep. Snoring is not usually life threatening - although it can be, but snoring can wake you up, will often wake up others, and can cause you to thoroughly embarrass yourself if you do it during class.

Snoring is caused by an obstruction in the airway. When the airway is clear, there is nothing for the air to vibrate against. However, if the airway is narrowed or partially blocked, the air going to and from the lungs will cause a vibration, and that vibration results in the snoring sound. Everyone gets a cold from time to time, and phlegm and mucus (snot) in the airway is a common cause of snoring; lying on one's back and having the mucus drain will increase the likelihood of snoring. Those people with allergies or who live in a dusty climate are more likely to have mucus, and therefore are more likely to snore.

Snoring can also be the sound of tissue vibrating; the looser the tissue is in one's throat, the more likely one is to snore. The throat tissue can be relaxed chemically by alcohol or sleeping pills or it can come about naturally due to age; therefore, people who drink before bed or are getting up in age are the most likely to snore. Adding extra tissue also makes the throat flabby and gives the air something to vibrate off; therefore, it should come as no surprise to learn that overweight people are more likely to snore than the general population.

Although weight can be controlled, some bodily features that incline one to snore cannot. People with large tongues, big nostrils, and/or a large uvula (that thing that hangs down in your throat) are built to snore.

Snoring is generally not harmful, but it is a sign that the airway is obstructed. If you wake up gasping and choking and the people around you say you were snoring very loudly, you should ask your doctor about it. Should the airway get clogged and remain clogged, you have what doctors call obstructive sleep apnea and, if the airway stays clogged for an extended period, you could suffocate. Constantly waking up from sleep startled having breathing issues is serious, but normal snoring is nothing to worry about.

FUN FACTS

Men are twice as likely to snore as women.

Nasal strips do help stop snoring because they lift the muscles in the nose, allowing more oxygen and preventing the muscle flab from vibrating.

Sleeping with your head on two pillows helps keep your sinuses from draining and reduces snoring.

People who sleep well tend to be in better moods than people who don't.

Smoke will irritate the throat tissues, making it likely that when air passes over them they will vibrate; hence, if you smoke cigarettes or other products or are around second-hand smoke, you are more likely to snore than a non-smoker.

Are you left-handed or right-handed? If I were to guess, I would say right-handed. Nine out of ten people reading this book are right-handed; only about ten percent of the human population is left-handed. Hearing that a minority of people are left-handed makes me wonder: Are these left-handed people some kind of freaks, are they the human race of the future, and did they have any control over choosing not to be right-handed or was it genetically wired into them?

Any time one is a minority – be it due to race, gender, or handedness, one is likely to be beaten down by the majority. In the past, left-handed people have been thought to have had the devil inside them, to be mentally ill, or to be inclined to be criminals, and therefore they have been shunned. Today, lefties still face discrimination, but it is usually much more subtle; for instance, a school district may not buy left-handed desks or left-handed scissors, a teacher may only teach the students how to write right-handed, and drinking fountains must be turned on by right hands. Because of society's conditioning, natural lefties are often comfortable using both hands, although they may use neither exceptionally well.

Your dominant hand is genetically wired into you. Researchers have found that babies in the womb already have a dominant hand choice. (A child will suck the thumb of the dominant hand both in the womb and out of the womb.) If you are a twin, you have a much greater chance of being a lefty than a non-twin. Hand-choice is determined by nature, not by how one is raised. Of course, if one is taught to do everything right-handed, one will get into the habit of being right-handed; however, give that person a new task and you will observe that person's true hand preference.

Don't believe everything you read about left-handed people. For instance, you may have read that they are creative; they are, but so are right-handed people. All people are creative, and, if you are using not being left-handed as an excuse for not being creative, you are only fooling yourself. Although past generations have been taught that left-handed people are primarily creative and right-handed people are primarily logical, modern research has debunked that theory. Until 2017, researchers believed that the gene for which hand dominates was found in the brain, but in 2017 researchers concluded it was in the spinal cord.

If you are a lefty, you do have one advantage. Unless you tell them differently, people will assume that you are right-handed, and this assumption enables many lefties to take their opponents in sports such as tennis, boxing, and baseball by surprise. If people already know you are a lefty, you won't have the advantage of surprise, but you will still have an advantage in sports because you have likely played right-handed people before; whereas many of your opponents will have never played a lefty and will have a hard time adapting to you.

FUN FACTS

The English word "left" is from the Anglo-Saxon word for weak, "lyft"; the left hand was the weaker hand in ancient societies just as it is in societies today.

Men are four percent more likely to be lefties than women.

Famous lefties include Albert Einstein, Benjamin Franklin, President Barack Obama, and King George VI of England.

Apes and many non-human mammals have about a fifty-fifty split between those who are right-handed and those who are left-handed.

No human society has more left-handed people than right-handed people.

WHY DO WE HICCUP?

The other day when I had the hiccups, a well-intentioned soul suggested, "Try holding your breath. It will cure hiccups." I thought to myself, holding your breath will stop everything if I hold it long enough. People seem to have all sorts of ideas about how to cure hiccups, but I wonder if many even know what hiccups are?

Hiccups are caused by the diaphragm muscle spasming uncontrollably. The diaphragm muscle is the muscle that we use when speaking; it helps us breath in and out. When the diaphragm muscle contracts, it causes the vocal cords to make a hiccup sound as they close.

Almost everyone has had hiccups; even babies in the womb get hiccups. Hiccups are caused by eating too fast or eating too much. Drinking alcohol or carbonated beverages can cause them; in cartoons, people who are intoxicated are often hiccupping. Eating and drinking are not the only reason for hiccups, though; being under stress can cause them and so can abrupt changes in temperature, such as going into a walk-in freezer after being in a hot restaurant kitchen.

Hiccups generally last only a few minutes, and, provided you can handle the embarrassment of having them, they will go away on their own. Even if they don't go away immediately, remain calm. If you have hiccups more than 48 hours straight – that's two consecutive days - then you should consider going to the doctor.

Lots of wisdom has been passed through the ages of how to get rid of hiccups. Most of these techniques aren't scientifically proven to work, but different people find that different techniques work for them. The kind soul who told me to hold my breath actually meant, "Take a deep breath of air and hold it for ten to twenty seconds, and then breathe out slowly. If that doesn't work, try it again." This is one of the many techniques that have worked for some people and have therefore been passed along to future generations; there is no one technique that works every time for everyone.

The technique of holding one's breath is designed to control breathing; it can get rid of hiccups by impacting the diaphragm. Other techniques eliminate hiccups by stimulating the muscles and nerves of the throat. For instance, next time you have the hiccups, try to grab the tip of your tongue, and pull it from your mouth. You can also try to stimulate the throat by drinking a glass of water quickly.

FUN FACTS

Almost all mammals get hiccups; yes, your dog can get hiccups.

One person had hiccups for 68 years.

If you feel embarrassed telling your teacher you have "the hiccups", tell your teacher that you have a case of "singultus", the official medical term for hiccups.

Hiccups generally occur between four and sixty per minute.

The Greek philosopher Plato is credited with being the first to write remedies for hiccups.

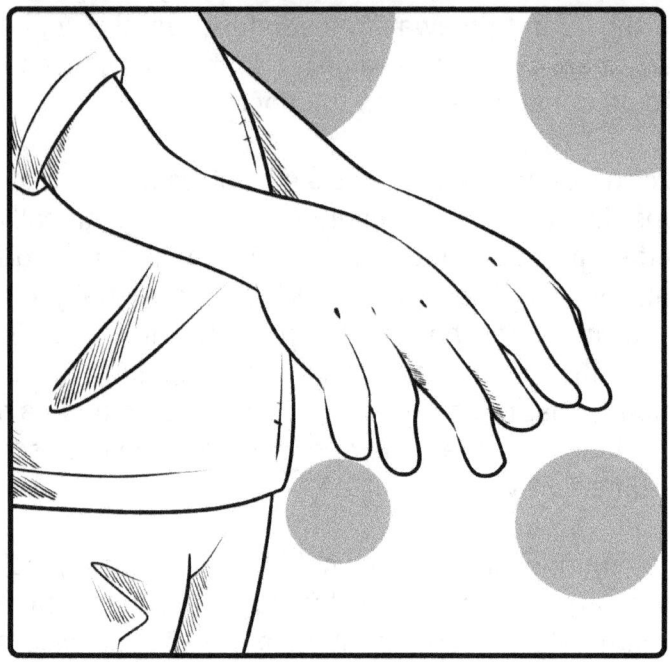

Before reading this article, let's do a couple of simple exercises. Open your hand – whichever one you want – and then take your thumb and touch your fingers one at a time. Next, put your hand into a fist.

We are the only living creatures that can do these exercises. Monkeys can't, and fish certainly can't! The fact that your thumb can comfortably touch each of your fingers allows you to grip with your thumb. The fact that your fingers, although different lengths, fold into your palm in a nice row to make a fist, which is then given additional support by the thumb, provides a weapon no other living being has.

Humans haven't always had the type of hands that we have today. The modern human hand appeared in evolution about a million years ago – sometimes between 800,000 – 1,400,000 years to be a little more technical. Prior to that, humans were walking around on their knuckles and had curved fingers like what chimpanzees have today. Whereas the chimpanzee-like hands were great for swinging on trees, the modern hand was good for gripping tools. Primitive people had become tool workers, and their DNA adjusted for the toolmaking, giving humans fatty pads in their palms that enable gripping; also, humans have three muscles in their thumbs that chimpanzees do not have. (If you don't believe in the theory of evolution and the survival-of-the-fittest – and they are just theories, at least admit that if a cook constantly puts his fingers on the grill, his fingers are going to get calloused so that he no longer feels the pain. You can't deny that the human body adjusts for the conditions in which it finds itself.)

The fingers and thumb work together to accomplish a wide range of tasks. The hand can do something very tedious one moment, such as thread a needle, and then do something very powerful the next moment, such as swing an ax. Because our fingers are different sizes, we can place our entire hand around a jar lid, giving us a much better grip than if all the fingers were the same size. Also, we can also throw things, such as a baseball or a rock, with much greater accuracy.

Will human hands always look the same as ours look today? Time will tell. At first our fingers being different lengths look like an evolutionary mistake, but, upon consideration, our bodies are very fit for the world in which we find ourselves. Future generations, too, will likely have hands shaped in whatever form that enables them to succeed in their environment.

FUN FACTS

Because the thumb and the fingers come to grip an item from different directions, they are "opposable", and, in this case, opposites really do attract.

Some anatomists – people who study the human body – claim that the thumb is not a finger; they say that the body has four fingers and a thumb. Others, though, claim that people have five fingers.

Beginning with the thumb and moving across the hand, the fingers are called "index", "middle", "ring", and "pinky".

Every finger has value, but, because the thumb is the only opposed to the rest, it is generally considered the most valuable.

Your palms and the underside of your fingers will not tan.

If you have ever taken the time to compare yourself to your dog, cat, or pretty much any other mammal you have come into contact with, you have likely noticed that you have far less hair than they do. Ever wonder why that is?

Primitive people were a lot hairier than we are, so the simple answer is "evolution". But why did evolution choose humans to lose hair? We are the only primates to be almost hairless.

We are not the only almost-hairless mammals, though. Elephants, rhinoceroses, and hippopotamuses are all almost-hairless too. These are huge animals who, like people, have lost their hair over generations. The elephant, for instance, descended from the wooly mammoth. These are big animals who live in hot places, and hair would keep the heat on their bodies. Hair holds heat. Their bodies and our bodies lost hair and developed sweat glands as a means of regulating body temperature.

Other almost-hairless mammals include the naked mole rat and the whale. In these cases, to be able to glide through the dirt and water, respectively, required smooth skin. Perhaps like these submerged beings, early people spent time gliding in the water, having all but the top of their heads under the water. The hair on their head, meanwhile, protected them from the sun.

Besides being comfortable on both land and water, early humans were also hunters. When people began to crave meat to supplement their diet of plants, they became hunters, and those bodies adapted toward hunting were most successful in carrying on the human species. Whereas chimpanzees continued to swing from tree to tree, people began to run to chase their prey. These early modern humans exerted a lot more bursts of energy than monkeys, and therefore their bodies had to keep their body temperature cool. Losing their hair and developing sweat glands was the best way to do this.

Because humans developed the ability to sweat profusely, they now had the ability to grow a bigger brain. Hair loss was not the only factor in why the human brain has evolved as it has – diet also made a difference, but hair loss is a major contributing factor.

Of course, being nearly hairless has its cons too. For instance, when we get scared, the hairs on our arms, legs, and back stand on end just like the hairs on a cat, dog, chimpanzee, and most other mammals do, but the hairs on us are so few and so thin that most people cannot see them. Also, we have no camouflage such as the leopard, zebra, and most other mammals; we cannot naturally blend into our surroundings. Thanks to clothes and body paints, though, we can camouflage ourselves and blend into our surroundings, whether it is a trip into the woods, a day at school, or a sports competition.

FUN FACTS

Red is the least common of all natural hair colors; only about 2% of humans have it.

The most common color of hair in humans is black.

The hair on your head will live for two to seven years before shedding. In about three months, the root will likely begin sprouting another strand.

You will lose 50 to 100 head hairs today. (That sounds bad, but you have approximately 100,000 head hair follicles, and each can produce numerous hairs.)

Hair does not turn gray; that gray coloring you see on older adults is the absence of pigment in the hair shaft.

If you have ever kept your body in water for an extended period – it might have been swimming in a pool, soaking in a tub, washing dishes, or even being sprayed by a showerhead, then you have likely experienced your fingertips and toes shriveling until they look like prunes. (If you're a fun-loving prankster like me, you are appalled by how you look, but you can't help calling attention to your prune-like digits in the hopes of grossing someone out.)

Believe it or not, those pruny digits you are seeing is your body making changes to adjust to the water. Whereas normally your fingertips are nice and smooth, they become wrinkled in the water. The wrinkles give your fingers a rougher texture which enhances your ability to pick up wet objects by or in the water, just as the tread on tires enables cars to better grip the wet road. The wrinkles cause the water to flow off your skin. If you were to live in the water instead of on land, the wrinkled texture would become your normal day-to-day texture, and should humans live in water for several generations, being born with wrinkled fingers would become commonplace. Wrinkled skin is an adaptation the body makes to enable it to better thrive in the wet environment.

The body creates the wrinkled texture by reducing the blood flow to the capillaries that run through one's fingers and toes. Early researchers believed that the wrinkles appeared because the body was taking in water through osmosis, but that has been disproven; people without nerve endings do not shrivel up, and, if the wrinkling was due to the intake of water, they would. Today's researchers know that our nerve endings send a message to our capillaries to become smaller; this constriction results in our wrinkles.

Although having one's hands in water is by far the most common reason people have prune-like fingers, other reasons also exist. For instance, if you do not drink enough water, your body will become dehydrated, and you will get prune-like fingers. Pruney fingers are just one sign of dehydration, though; if you have dehydration, you will also have other symptoms such as a dry mouth, feeling dizzy, and dark yellow urine.

Pruney fingers resulting from being in water may be gross looking, but they are nothing to worry about. Once your hands are removed from the water, your normal blood flow will return, and your body will carry on as usual. Although you could damage your skin if you kept your fingers in a wrinkled state for weeks, you won't damage your skin if it stays wrinkled for a few hours. Overall, wrinkled fingers are nothing serious; they are just evidence of the body trying to adjust to a new environment.

FUN FACTS

The skin on one's fingertips and bottoms of one's toes is smooth and hairless; the technical term for this is "glabrous".

Water cannot flow into the skin. (If you don't believe me, place a drop of water on your skin and wait – it will disappear because of evaporation but not because of soaking into the skin.)

The only parts of the body to wrinkle in water are the fingers and the toes; this could be because they are the only parts of the body that grip objects.

Your skin is your body's largest organ.

Skin serves a variety of functions besides making you look charming – it enables the sense of touch, it cools the body, it protects the body from germs, and it allows movement.

Look at your fingernails and your toenails.

If you trimmed all your nails at the same time recently, you may be amazed to discover that your fingernails have grown almost twice or even three times as much as your toenails have. On the other hand (no pun intended), if you have a pet or other critter with nails, you have probably observed that their nails all grow at the same pace.

This usual growth rate can be explained by how we use our digits. People use their fingernails much more than they use their toenails. This use causes trauma to the nail, and so the body rushes oxygen and nutrients to the nail. As I pound on the keyboard keys typing this book for you, my fingernails are being traumatized; if you pause to think about it, your nails too likely take a lot of abuse during the day.

As you might suspect, the more a finger is used, the more the nail of that finger will grow. Hold your two hands in front of you and look at the nails on each hand. The nails on your dominant hand are likely longer than the nails on your nondominant one; this is because you have used your dominant hand more. Now, look at the fingers on your dominant hand. The chances are that your little finger's nail has grown the least of the five; this is because you use your littlest finger the least.

Believe it or not, clipping your nails, just like pruning a plant, will lead to your nails growing faster than they would if you did nothing. The clipping causes trauma to the nail, and that inspires the body to provide extra oxygen and nutrients to it. (Biting your nails will also cause them to grow faster, and it is a "bad habit" many nervous people have. Although the nail itself contains no chemical that would hurt you, nails often have germs under them and therefore can make you sick.)

Trauma is the main reason nails grow, but other reasons also exist. Teenagers and women who are pregnant grow nails faster than the average person; this is because of the hormones that are raging through their bodies. The weather can make a difference too; for instance, people tend to grow nails the fastest during the hot summer months. Even genealogy makes a difference; if your parents both have nails that grow fast, you will too.

FUN FACTS

Your fingernails grow approximately 1/10 of a millimeter per day, approximately 3.4 millimeters per month; that's one-tenth of an inch per month.

Because of poor circulation problems, elderly people's nails grow slower than the average person's nails.

The white, half-moon shape at the bottom of your fingers is known as the lunula.

The same material that comprises your fingernail, the protein alpha-keratin, is found in one's hair as well. It is also found in the hooves, horns, and claws of other animals.

Men tend to grow nails faster than women; the exception is when a woman is pregnant.

WHY ARE OUR LIPS PINK?

Have you ever noticed that all healthy people, regardless of their race or gender, have pink lips? Ever wonder why? The answer is literally right underneath your nose.

Lips are skin. However, compared to the other skin on you, the lips are thin. Many layers of the outer skin are missing. These missing layers provide your body with melanin elsewhere; melanin is the chemical that gives your skin color. These missing skin layers also mean that the red blood cells are much closer to the surface than they are in most places; that red coloring is the red blood cells.

Lips have been essential in human development. Like all mammals, infant humans know how to use their lips to latch onto a nipple to obtain nourishment. The fact that the lip's skin is thin means the nerve endings are very close to the surface, making this something pleasurable, reinforcing the behavior.

Lip pressing, putting one's lips on the lips of someone else –

kissing, for those readers who don't appreciate euphemisms, likely began as a form of biological necessity. That's right, kissing between mother and children may have evolved as a way for toddlers to survive. Before the days of baby food jars being available at the local supermarket, a mother would chew the infant's food and then pass it through her lips to her infant. This was an act of love that both the toddler and the mother could enjoy both physically and emotionally.

Not all living creatures have lips – think of birds and turtles for example. Of all the many animals that do have lips, humans are unique because our lips purse outward instead of inward. This partially explains why humans can vocalize so many different sounds whereas other creatures cannot. Our lips also help us express ourselves nonverbally through gestures; for instance, a surprised person will open their lips into a huge "O" shape.

Our lips reveal a lot about our health. Pink lips are the norm; pink lips have red blood cells pulsating through them as they should. Lips can be other colors than pink, though. If someone has candy-apple red lips, their liver may not be working right. If their lips are white, they may be dehydrated. If their lips are blue, they may be cold. Always remember if your lips are any color but pink, you need to take precautions and likely talk to the school nurse or other health professional. We may take our lips for granted, but they play a key role in the survival of the species.

FUN FACTS

Human lips get thinner as people get older.

One kiss passes approximately 300 bacteria.

A full minute of kissing will burn approximately 26 calories.

The lips are the most sensitive organ of the body. They have approximately one million nerve endings and no way to protect them.

Do you have dry lips? The lips have no sweat glands, and therefore they dry out before any other spot in the body.

WHY DO MOST TEENAGERS GET PIMPLES?

Skin experts – dermatologists – say that we should not pick our pimples. I'll confess, though, I have picked mine more than once. I have watched a white squiggly line come out of a pimple just as if it were toothpaste being squeezed from a toothpaste tube. I have also had hard kernels fly from the pimple, as well as gotten covered in a fountain of white goo. I don't want to gross you out if you are among the lucky 15% who have never experienced any of these, but the other 85% of the people reading this book can likely relate to having pimples – and even if you don't have pimples you likely have probably a friend or two who does.

First, the good news: Acne is not contagious. You can hang around your zit-faced friends and not catch it from them. More good news: There is only one way to get acne; here's how: The oil glands on your face will produce more oil than your body needs; the oil mixes with dead skin cells and blocks your pores and hair follicles, creating the perfect breeding ground for bacteria. When bacteria grow in your clogged pores and hair follicles, the result is an outbreak of pimples. That – and that alone – is the only way to get acne.

Now the bad news: as your body changes, it is very, very, very likely to overproduce oil, setting in motion the chain of events that result in bacteria settling into your pores. Oil is a good thing in moderation – it adds softness to hair, and it lubricates the skin; however, too much oil leads to pimples. Overproduction of oil happens a lot during one's teen years – that's why pimples are associated with teens. Almost half of all teenagers will have had a serious round or more of acne before they reach their mid-teens. You may get lucky and not get pimples as a teen, but don't be surprised if you get them later. People of all ages can get acne, and over 85% of the population will have had it by the time they are aged fifty. Needless to say, acne is a very common skin disorder in all cultures, and in the United States, it is the most common skin ailment.

"Pimples" is a broad term covering six more specific terms; it is possible to have more than one form of pimples at the same time, and most people encounter each of the six forms during their life: blackheads and white heads are slightly raised bumps that have a head; if the head is under the skin it is white and if it is outside the skin it is black because the head oxidizes; papules and pustules are both are red, tender lumps and the latter have pus in them; and both nodules and cysts are deep, large, and very sore, and the latter have pus in them.

Pus is the white goo that pops from the pimple; of the six forms of pimples, only two forms- pustules and cysts - have pus. Pus is composed of dead tissue, cells, and bacteria. Skin doctors recommend that these not be messed with, especially in the case of cysts.

FUN FACTS

Outbreaks of pimples come and go for most people. Women's hormones, especially, shift during the month, at times causing the body to produce more oil than others and thereby creating an outbreak of pimples. Once the hormones change back, the extra oil ceases and the outbreak disappears.

Despite numerous attempts to prove otherwise, chocolate, fries, and pizza have not been scientifically proven to cause acne.

Periodic doses of 10 to 20 minutes of exposure to the sun helps minimize pimples breaking out.

Washing your face more than twice per day can be as hard on it as not washing it enough.

Squeeze the skin on your nose. Do you have any "sebaceous filament"? Sebaceous filament is the thin stringy stuff that pops out of your pores when you squeeze your nose.

PART 3

NATURE

🪴 **PLANTS**

🐾 **ANIMALS**

🌧️ **WEATHER**

WHY DO RABBITS WIGGLE THEIR NOSES?

Can you wiggle your nose like a rabbit? Some people can; some people can't. All rabbits, though, wiggle their nose constantly. Have you ever wondered why?

Rabbits, like humans, have five senses – sight, sound, touch, taste, and smell. Whereas we humans tend to rely on sight and sound, rabbits rely greatly on smell. When they raise their nasal passage, they can smell more, and the more they smell, the more attuned they are to the world around them.

Raising the nasal passage is not the only way a rabbit can heighten the sense of smell; the rabbit can also wiggle its nose at a greater speed. The faster a rabbit wiggles its nose, the more sensory receptors that are exposed. The rabbit has over 100 million receptors. (That sounds like a lot, but don't forget that we are bigger than rabbits, and therefore it shouldn't surprise you to learn that you and I have approximately 220 million.) If you see a rabbit with its nasal passage raised and its nose wiggling fast, then you know the rabbit is on high alert.

The twitching of a rabbit's nose means that it is looking for more information; you will certainly see it twitch if it suspects that a predator is nearby. However, predators are not the only thing a rabbit seeks information about. If you acquire a pet rabbit, don't be surprised that the rabbit sniffs you when you are introduced; the rabbit will memorize your scent and associate that scent as something pleasant. Rabbits will also sniff when they want to know about the environment, such as where the closest food source is. Rabbits are very curious animals, and they want to learn about the world around them for a variety of reasons; therefore, since they are nearly always collecting data about their environment, their noses are constantly twitching.

FUN FACTS

Although rabbits use their nose, a rabbit has 360-degree vision; that is, it can see all around itself.

A rabbit uses its whiskers as dust filters to keep debris out of its nostrils.

A rabbit uses its nostrils to regulate its body temperature, and if it is too hot or too cold it will adjust its nostril size.

The stronger a scent is, the moister the inside of the rabbit's nose becomes.

A rabbit's nose will constantly move; if it is not moving, the normally curious, alert creature is feeling sick, sad, or stressed.

WHY DO FISH LIVE IN SCHOOLS?

Fish live in schools. No, silly, I don't mean that they reside in a building where the A-B-Cs and 1-2-3s are taught; I mean that they live as a group. Fish live with other fish of the same species in groups of four to thousands, and this group is called a "school". (Similarly, cattle live in a "herd", geese live in a "gaggle", and crows live in a "murder".)

To be clear, only about 25% of the world's fish live in schools, and these fish that do live in schools are usually small fish. Being in a school offers many advantages to being on one's own. he main attraction is safety. Just as bullies are likely to leave you alone if you are in a group, fish know there is safety in numbers. A lone fish can be easy prey, but a group of fish can band together to escape a predator.

Fish swim in groups to not only protect their own lives, but also the lives of the next generation. Many predators like fish eggs, and a lone fish can do little to protect those eggs. However, fish that release eggs in large groups can try to protect the eggs and, by working together, ensure that some of the eggs survive and hatch. Small fish that are in schools are more likely to carry on the species; therefore, most small fish are genetically programmed to seek schools.

A third advantage to living in a school is finding food. If any member of the school finds a food source, the whole school can enjoy the food. The odds of finding food in a group with numerous eyes looking is much better than one fish relying on just its own two eyes.

Being together in the school also aids in communication. I am guessing that you tend to stand within about four feet of a person you are talking to; being that close enables you to listen to each other and hear each other more clearly than if you were far apart. The same principles apply to fish. Fish communicate through movement and sounds, so the closer they are to one another, the clearer the message.

FUN FACTS

Piranhas, one of the meanest fish in the world, don't need protection, but they still travel in schools for advantages like finding food.

If a school of fish is under attack, the school will often swim in a circle so that the predator becomes confused.

Fish can learn. For instance, if you always put fish food in the same spot in a fish tank, the fish will learn to go there when it is hungry.

Fish change positions in the school; hence the back fish gets a turn at being the lead fish.

Just as some humans stay around their hometown after graduating high school and others go to other places, some fish stay in the same school all their lives, but others change groups periodically during their lifetime.

WHY ARE FLIES ATTRACTED TO POOP?

Whether you are in a pasture at a farm or are walking a dog in the park, if you find a pile of fresh poop, you are likely to find flies. There is no denying it! Just as a magnet attracts metal, poop draws flies!

Poop smells to a fly the way expensive perfume smells to us. Much poop is buried deep within grass – we can't see it and the fly can't see it, the odor coming from the poop clues the fly that the poop exists. Like the music from the flute of the Pied Piper, the smell grabs and holds the fly's attention, guiding the fly to it.

Poop is more than just an aromatic pleasure for the fly; poop is a food source for flies. Poop contains proteins, fats, carbohydrates, minerals, and bacteria – both living and dead - that benefit the flies' diet. Poop has great nutritional value for flies.

Flies love the taste of poop. Rotting food and dead animals attract them too, but poop is the favorite meal of most flies. Flies taste with their feet – their taste buds are in their feet and not their mouths – and therefore they walk all over their food as they eat it. (Flies are extremely germy because of this.)

Flies also find fresh poop to be the ideal place to lay one's eggs. Fresh poop is warm and moist, and this keeps the eggs warm and provides nutrition for them. Fly eggs hatch within 24 hours, and the baby flies - maggots, they often look like living grains of white rice - eat the poop they have been born in. After four days of feasting as a maggot, the larvae will leave the poop to spend the next four days morphing into a fly.

Within a few hours of being a fly, the female fly is ready to scout out a new pile of fresh poop and begin the reproductive cycle all over again.

FUN FACTS

The expression, "like flies on poop" compares how enthusiastic a person is to do something to how flies are naturally attracted to poop.

Although poop has nutritional value for flies, it has none for humans.

Flies aren't the only ones who eat poop; beetles, butterflies, and other insects do as well.

Some flies prefer fruit, meat, and nectar to poop; houseflies – the type of fly you are most likely to see, though, prefer poop.

Flies can detect poop that is over four miles away!

My mom likes to dress our family dog in a sweater in the wintertime. She believes that it helps to keep the dog warm on chilly days, provides atmosphere during the Christmas season, and creates a conversation piece for visitors. Walk into almost any pet shop, and you will see costumes for our canine friends. What you will seldom see, though, is jewelry.

Go out into the country on a cold winter day, though, and you will find cattle with wrap−around blankets − and nose rings. The wrap-around blankets are understandable; they are to keep the cattle warm. The purpose of the nose ring − which is worn year-round by some cattle − is a mystery to most people.

The nose-ring is not a fashion statement; it has two very practical purposes. One, it weans the younger cattle off their mom's milk. A strategically placed ring makes getting to the udder very difficult and/or painful on both the calf and the mom − especially if the nose ring has a spike that is stabbing the mother in the udder. Two, the ring provides a way for the farmer to better control the animal. By tugging on the ring with a steel tube or by putting a rope through the ring and tugging on the rope, the animal will go the direction the farmer wants. The nose ring can even save a farmer's life; by grabbing the nose ring when a bull is becoming aggressive, the farmer can convince the bull to settle down. Nose rings that are for weaning are temporary, but nose rings that are placed for controlling behavior are generally permanent.

Nose rings are put into the cattle's nose with a device called "nose tongs", and nose rings are removed with the same device. The nose ring does not pierce the cattle's septum, but clamps to each side of it inside the nostril. The cattle are usually scared and angry throughout the installation procedure, so experienced veterinarians are typically called upon to install the nose ring. Veterinarians also have access to both anesthesia and healing ointment, two things that can greatly reduce the cattle's agony during and after the procedure.

FUN FACTS

Dairy cows may not be vicious like bulls, but many have nose rings to aid in the farmer controlling them during the milking process.

Installing a nose ring is risky to the cattle's health; cattle can develop an infection and possibly die.

The average nose ring is 3-5 inches in diameter.

Human nose rings often have symbolic meaning; nose rings on cattle carry no culture-specific meaning.

The cattle's noses are more sensitive to pain than their ears are; since the purpose of the nose ring is to create pain to obtain the behavior the farmer wants, the more sensitive nose is the logical place to place it.

WHY DO DOGS TURN AROUND AND AROUND BEFORE LYING DOWN?

Dogs may be man's (and woman's) best friend, but they certainly have some strange quirks about them. One quirk you have probably seen but may have not thought about is spinning in a circle before lying down. This behavior inspired one of my dad's favorite jokes:

Son: Why did you name our dogs Timex and Rolex?
Dad: Because they are watchdogs.
Son: Them? They don't guard anything.
Dad: They always wind themselves up every night before bed.

My dad has a quirky sense of humor, I admit, but he does have a point; most dogs turn in circles before lying down.

Scientists have found several reasons for this odd behavior. One, it is a survival skill passed through DNA. Just as a baby human has been pre-programmed to know how to suck to get milk from a nipple, dogs have been pre-programmed to turn around in circles.

When a dog walks in circles at bedtime, it is doing what comes naturally. It is an unconscious behavior. If you were to ask your dog why it does it, you would get a reply such as, "Doesn't everybody?"

Walking around in circles was a survival defense when dogs lived in the wild. By walking in circles, the dog can see if any predators are nearby. Having spun around a few times and not seen any danger, the dog can lie down knowing it is safe. Still, to protect its vulnerable underside, a dog will often curl into a ball so that its tail and head are close together.

A second practical reason for this odd behavior also exists. In the wild, grass grows tall. Trampling the grass with one's feet makes the ground softer; the grass provides a cushion. Even though the dog may have a bed, it still has and follows the instinct to turn around.

A third practical reason is that the trampled grass bed reserves one's spot. Just as if we were to go camping and see somebody else's tent set up, we would move on; when a second dog sees the trampled grass, it knows the area has been claimed. From leaving a jacket on one's chair or a receipt on one's dinner table when one goes to a buffet, humans mark their territory with items all the time, so it should come as no surprise that other mammals do as well.

FUN FACTS

The first animal to be domesticated was the wolf dog; this occurred over 15,000 years ago.

Dogs have been domesticated and can handle numerous chores, including guarding possessions, sniff out the trail of a lost person, pull sleds, flush quail, guide the blind, and point out prey.

Smaller breeds of dogs sleep less than larger breeds.

Dogs dream while sleeping.

Dogs can experience insomnia, not being able to go to sleep.

Have you ever assumed that a gesture meant one thing and then found out later that it meant something else. For instance, the other day in class a girl had her hand up in the air. Typically, hands are up in a classroom because someone knows an answer to a question. She explained hers was up so that her fingernail polish would dry.

It's easy to misread animal gestures too. I'm guessing that sometime in your life a cat – it may have been one that you knew well, or it may have been a stranger – came over to you and itched its back by rubbing against your leg. If you're like me, you attributed that to an itch, and to oneself being a human scratching post. If so, you misread the gesture.

The cat was likely claiming you. Like a male dog marking its territory with drops of urine, a cat will mark its territory by releasing a scent upon it. If a cat puts its scent on you, you are its friend. Just as humans shake hands when they see a friend, cats that like each other put their scents on each other.

If it is a cat that you know well, this was likely the first of several nonverbal behaviors it displayed. The cat was not only claiming you as its own, but it was also trying to get your attention. It likely wanted you to acknowledge it or to feed it; that cat was wanting you to take a particular action.

Rubbing against you feels good both physically and psychologically for the cat. Hopefully, you too feel positive energy from the encounter. If you don't, you can break your cat from rubbing on you by not rewarding the rubbing behavior and by rewarding an alternative behavior instead – both verbally and with cat treats. Cats hate the smell of citrus, so spray yourself with some lemon scented detergent or simply cover yourself in orange peels, and the cat will likely keep away. Cats have the same IQ as a human toddler, and they will quickly adapt to the behavior you prefer.

FUN FACTS

Cats lick themselves to get rid of scents.

The cat's sense of smell is 14 times better than humans and surpasses most dogs.

A cat can arch its back because it has 53 loose fitting vertebrae in its spine.

The technical word for a cat rubbing its head on you to get its scent on you and claim you as its own is "bunting".

Kittens tend to learn socialization around humans between age 3-9 weeks. The kittens will watch how you treat their mother. What you do during this time will greatly determine the bond you will have with the kittens for the rest of their lives.

WHY DO CATS SIT ON MOUNDS OF CLOTHES?

Out of all the places in the house to lie – sofas, beds, rugs – why do cats – and sometimes dogs - so often choose to lie on a pile of clothes? Is it just to irritate you?

Believe it or not, the answer to this question can be yes. Sometimes your cat wants your attention, and if you won't give it attention for positive behavior, it will do things to provoke you, such as getting cat hair on your clean laundry. Sometimes this misbehavior is cute, such as hiding in your shoe, and sometimes it is disgusting, such as using your bed as a litter box. If your cat is on the clothes and exhibiting attention-getting behavior, you have found your explanation of why the cat is on your clothes.

If you don't see any of these other passive-aggressive behaviors, though, your cat is likely there because the cat found lying on the clothes to be a very pleasurable experience. Remember the proverb, "curiosity killed the cat"? Cats get on your mountain of laundry because they want to feel the textures; they are curious about what the clothing feels like. They also want to check out the view from the top. Also, the laundry may not only look inviting, but if they are cool, they want to see if the clothing can provide warmth for them.

A cat's sense of smell is 14 times greater than that of a human. Although you may not want to hear it, you have a distinct odor about you, an odor your cat can recognize. Your clothes pick up that odor – and even if they are freshly washed they often retain remnants of that odor, so when a cat sits on your clothes, it gets to smell you even if you aren't there. Talk about aromatherapy! At the opposite extreme, your cat emits odors too. Cats have scent glands in their paws. If your mountain of laundry impressed your cat, it is likely marking that pile as its own territory by using its glands. In fact, your odor mixed with the cat's odor creates a unique blend of odors, one of your cat's favorite smells.

FUN FACTS

Cats are not native to North America. They were introduced to North and South America by Europeans who wanted to get rid of pests.

Researchers believe that cats have excellent hearing, know their name, and understand simple commands; however, they have concluded cats only choose to respond to human commands and requests about 10% of the time.

Cats are currently more popular than dogs as pets in the United States; there are over 88 million domesticated cats.

How many hairs could a cat put on your clothes? The typical cat has 130,000 hairs per square inch of its body. You do the math.

Cats have short attention spans. If you plan to train your cat, plan on no more than ten minutes per training session.

It's a fact that heat arises; the higher one goes, the warmer one gets. Therefore, one would expect to find snow on the ground but not at higher elevations. That would make sense. However, if you live near mountains, you know this is not true – most mountains have a snowy top much of the year. How can this be?

Let me share another fact: the closer one gets to the sun, the greater the heat. The temperature on Mercury is much greater than the temperature on Earth, and the temperature on Earth is much greater than the temperature on Neptune. Therefore, in my mind, it makes sense to expect to find snow down in the valleys but not on mountain tops; afterall, mountains are a whole lot closer to the sun than valleys. Again, though, a quick look at the Rocky Mountains and other mountain chains shows this is not the case. How can there be snow on mountain tops?

Believe it or not, a mountain is the coldest at the top. Part of this can be attributed to the fact that the earth has a hot core, and that the further one moves from the core, the cooler the temperature is going to get. The second fact, and the one that most people readily point to, is as one climbs up the mountain the air pressure decreases and the atmosphere gets thinner. This results in the temperature getting colder and colder as one goes up the mountain.

Some of the snow on the mountaintop comes from the recycling of previous snow, but a lot of the snow comes from lands near and far. Because it is so cool at the mountain top, not much evaporation is taking place. The water that is evaporated stays close to where it came from; moisture gets put into the air, stays in the air, and then falls back to the mountain top as rain or snow. Meanwhile, clouds of moisture that gathered in lands near and far are blowing across the sky. When they come to the mountain, they have to go up and over it – that's right, some mountains are taller than clouds. As the clouds go up, they cool, dropping much of their content, resulting in rain and snow on the mountain top.

The higher the elevation, the more likely a mountaintop will have snow. The highest elevations of all will have snow-topped mountains year-round. An individual mountain range may have a particular number of feet above sea level in which snow can be found on each peak – they call this "the snow line". Different ranges have different snow lines because they have different amounts of moisture. For instance, mountains found near the coast have a much lower snow line because of all the water that is in the air. Meanwhile, other mountains, such as the Andes in South America, are found in dry climates, and despite being really, really tall mountains, they are virtually moistureless.

FUN FACTS

Weather on a mountaintop can change drastically in less than an hour. If you ever hike a mountain, be prepared for some wild weather.

If there is a high wind and extreme cold on a mountain top, you will likely experience a blizzard.

Thanks to mountains, snow can be found near the equator.

Some mountains consist of a jungle at their bottom and – just a few miles higher – they have year-round ice.

Mountains can work like walls. If clouds are unable to get over the mountain, you'll see lush green land on one side and barren brown land on the other side.

WHY DO WE HAVE DIFFERENT TIME ZONES AROUND THE WORLD?

I have a friend who lives in the United Kingdom. When I am getting ready for supper, she is lying down to go to sleep. Why can't we all have the same time, so when it is 6 o'clock here in the United States, it is 11 o'clock there?

It's not just the United Kingdom that doesn't keep the same time as we do in my city. If you've ever been to a fancy hotel, you've probably seen clocks behind the front desk, showing that Tokyo, Japan is one time; Moscow, Russia, is another, and Paris, France, is yet another. Even here in the United States, not everybody shares my Kansas City, Missouri, time. The people in New York are an hour ahead of us, and the people in Los Angeles are two hours behind us. Why can't we all have the same time?

The reason could be perceived as egotistical – we all want to claim the time that the sun is at its peak as noon. The sun, though, reaches different communities at different times. When the sun is at its peak here in Kansas City, it is slowly working its way over the Rocky Mountains to the Pacific Ocean; it will take two hours to travel there, so my friends in California are still in their mid-morning part of the day.

Well, technically that is not true – the sun does not travel as the day progresses. People thought it was true until around 1650, but it was proven false. The sun does not move; the sun stands still. Everything else in the universe moves in relation to the sun. The earth spins around the sun; the sun does not spin around the earth. However, it does look like the sun is moving across the sky.

Every 24 hours, the earth makes one full rotation around the sun. That's what a day is; it is one full spin. It takes slightly over 365 spins for the earth to complete a trip around the sun; 365 spins comprise a year. (Every fourth year, an extra day is added to the calendar to accommodate that slight overage that is required to complete a full spin; hence we combine those four chunks of overage into one day, and we call that year with the extra day "leap year".)

Okay, math whizzes, here we go. How many degrees are in a circle? (If you said 360 you are correct.) By dividing 360 degrees by 24, we can determine how many degrees the earth rotates in an hour. (The answer is 15; every hour the earth spins 15 degrees.) It would make sense, then, that there would be 24 time zones. (There are actually more than 24 time zones because of politics. For instance, China, which is a huge country that would span six of the 15-degree time zones, has one time zone for its entire population.)

Time zones are important because they help the world communicate. A couple of hundred years ago, every village set its own time; it was possible for a train to leave from one town at noon and arrive at noon in the next town. With time zones, though, people had an idea of what the time was in the region; therefore, even though it may be frustrating that my friend in the United Kingdom is five hours ahead of me, I know with certainty she is five hours ahead. This certainty has allowed businesses, group projects, and other endeavors where people come from multiple countries to come together. If it wasn't for time zones, the global economy would not exist.

FUN FACTS

The time zones that are used worldwide today were first proposed by a Canadian engineer, Sir Sandford Fleming, in 1878. (In 1884, the International Prime Meridian Conference officially accepted them.)

Of all the nouns in the English language – a noun is a word that describes a person, place of thing, "time" is the most used.

Although the European part of France is within one time zone, France has world-wide possessions in twelve different time zones. The United Kingdom, meanwhile, is also within one time zone, but it has possession in nine different time zones.

The first device to determine noon was the sundial.

"Daylight Savings Time" is when people in one time zone set their clocks ahead one hour so there is more daylight in the evening. When not using Daylight Savings Time, people are on "Standard Time".

WHY DO LEAVES CHANGE COLORS IN AUTUMN?

If you live in a climate where the seasons are distinct – winter, spring, summer, and autumn, then you have likely witnessed the yellow, red, and orange beauty of leaves that occurs a couple of weeks before the leaves fall from the tree. For many people, it is the most gorgeous time of the entire year.

To better understand the colors that the leaves become, let's recall the color the leaves were originally – green. Leaves receive their green color from chlorophyll, a chemical which plants use to get food from sunlight. Chlorophyll absorbs red and blue wavelengths, and – if you remember the color wheel, yellow and blue make green. Therefore, when trees are making chlorophyll, their leaves are green. Trees with needles - pine trees for example - are green around the entire year; they can make chlorophyll year-round. Trees with big leaves, though, need lots of sunlight to make lots of leaf food, and, when the daylight starts to get shorter, they no longer need much chlorophyll since there is little sunlight to turn into food.

When the leaf stops producing chlorophyll, the green color fades, and other colors appear. The same chemical that gives corn its yellow color and carrots their orange color, carotenoid, is always in the leaf, but it is masked because the green is so thick. As the temperature drops, some leaves will react by turning red. The red coloring is not there all along; it is made by the tree in reaction to the cold weather. The reddest leaves – and the brightest colors overall - will be produced in years when the days are sunny, and the nights are cool. A leaf can be one color, a combination of different colors, or a blend of colors.

Because the trees cannot produce food for the leaves without sunlight, the trees put up a wall of cells to cut the leaves off from the sugar the tree produces. Once they are walled off, these leaves are no longer nourished; they are in essence cut off, and when a wind comes, they will fall to the ground. Those few leaves that don't get blown to the ground will eventually lose their pigment and turn brown.

By sacrificing its leaves, the tree will be able to convert enough sunlight, water, and carbon dioxide to keep itself alive during the winter. When spring comes and the days get longer, the tree will once again send out leaves. The leaves will bud and, as the days get longer, the tree will nourish them with chlorophyll, providing beautiful green leaves for all to enjoy.

Some trees have specific colors their leaves typically turn:

Aspen leaves are golden yellow.
Dogwood leaves are purplish red.
Hickory leaves are golden bronze.
Red maple leaves are scarlet.

If you look at a leaf carefully, you will see lines. The lines on the leaves are veins; the tree uses these to move fluids to and from the leaf.

Most trees change their leaves at the same time, but some trees, such as sourwood trees, are earlier than most, and others, such as oak trees, are later than average.

In the forest, fallen leaves provide food and fertilizer.

Although weather, temperature, and other variables make it impossible to predict exactly when trees will begin to change colors, in the United States in general the New England area leaves will start to turn colors in late September and the change of colors will advance Southward on a six-week trek as the weather gets cooler with the trees in South Carolina and Georgia turning colors in early November.

WHY ARE SOME STARS BRIGHTER THAN OTHER STARS?

Star light; star bright;
First star I see tonight.
I wish I may
I wish I might
Have the wish I wish tonight.

This nursery rhyme, which likely began in the United States around 1850, migrated to Great Britain, and then became worldwide, raises an interesting question – why are some stars brighter than others?

The stars are always shining. However, because of the brightness of one star, the sun - the sun is a star, and that particular star happens to be the center of our universe - we cannot always see these other stars.

How close a star is to Earth is one determinant of how bright it appears. The closer the star is, the brighter it will appear;

the closer the star is, the more light from the star that reaches our eyes.

Distance is just one factor, though, that determines how bright a star is. Stars are big balls of gas. Stars age over time, and they eventually burn out. (Yes, one day the sun is going to burn out, but it is nothing that we need to worry about because it is millions of years from happening.) Stars produce light because they are hot; however, some stars are hotter than others. Because they are at different temperatures, the type of light will vary. Stars that are the coolest – but still way too hot to touch - glow red; stars like the sun glow yellow; and extremely hot stars glow white or bluish-white.

A third factor determining a star's brightness is size. Just as seeing a boulder in the road is much easier than seeing a pebble there, seeing a big star in the sky is much easier than seeing a small star.

Astronomers have found over 100,000 different stars; they estimate there are billions of stars in the universe. Of the billions of stars that fill the universe, we see only the biggest, brightest, and closest.

FUN FACTS

Stars emit the same amount of light in every direction.

Hipparchus, a Greek living around 200 B.C.E., was the first known person to measure a star's light.

A star's light takes time to travel. When you see the sunlight, you see it as it was 8.5 minutes ago.

Sirius is the brightest star in our solar system. When you see its light, you see it as it was over eight years ago.

Stars shine brightest right before they burn out.

WHY DO WE WISH ON STARS?

Have you ever wished upon a star? People often make a wish on the first star they see on a particular evening or upon seeing a falling star.

Making a wish can be a simple process of merely thinking to oneself, "I wish that . . ." to a complex ritual. For instance, in the United States the ritual may involve stopping where one is, closing one's eyes, muttering a magical chant such as the "Star light, star bright" rhyme mentioned in the previous essay, and then committing oneself to never telling anyone what the wish was. Should one peak during the chanting or reveal what the wish was, the wish will not come true. People in other countries also wish on stars, but many have a different ritual. For instance, in Chile you must pick up a stone to hold as you make your wish upon a star.

Although some people believe in the power of stars and horoscopes, many people wish on stars merely for the entertainment value, just as they anxiously open their fortune cookie even though they don't believe a word they read. The skeptics have good reason not to expect their wish to come true; scientific studies have been conducted, and the data suggests that merely wishing on a star will not make a wish come true. However – believe it or not, wishing on a star, making a plan, and then working the plan will likely make the wish come true.

In the days before science, people did not understand nature or astronomy and were in great awe of the environment. A falling star, also known as a shooting star, was believed to be a star on its way to a god, and any wish made upon it would be taken to the god. Whereas ancients saw a falling star, today's scientists know that the so-called star is a falling meteorite burning up as it approaches earth.

Most people realize falling stars are just falling rocks and regular stars are just balls of gas, but people still make wishes on these just the same. Some people are still in awe of the heavens, and they believe there is a greater Being than they are. Even many of those who don't believe in gods, Fate, or a Keeper of the Stars still manage to believe enough to make a wish just in case they are wrong about the Heavens having no say in their lives. It can't hurt, can it?

FUN FACTS

If you can get away from the bright city lights and see a clear nighttime sky, you will likely see a falling star; over 48.5 tons of meteoroid material falls into earth's atmosphere every 24-hours.

If you wish upon a falling star in the Philippines, you must tie a knot in your handkerchief before the light disappears.

In many cultures, shooting stars represent souls on the move.

Wishing on stars is common in most human cultures.

Ancient Greeks believed shooting stars were the result of the king of the gods, Zeus, expressing frustration by throwing debris at the earth.

PART 4

BUSINESS AND COMMUNITY

WHY DO DOCTORS WEAR WHITE LAB COATS?

Around 1800, medical professionals could be classified into four groups. One group was the traditionalists, practitioners who believed in using leeches and other techniques that had been around for years. A second group was the superstitious spiritualists, healers who believed in divine cures and folk remedies. The third group was the quacks, the snake-oil salespeople, professional con artists who claimed to offer miracle cures to whatever ailments one had and knew that what they offered was merely a placebo. The fourth group was the scientists, doctors who believed that bacteria existed, who tested their hunches, and who used the latest evidence-based medicines. The public had a problem, though; they couldn't tell one type of doctor from the other types.

To resolve this issue, those doctors who valued medical science chose to wear the white lab coat of the scientist. Today, medical doctors typically receive a short lab apron when they begin their studies and a long lab apron when they graduate; regardless of whether a lab coat is long or short, when patients see someone in a white lab coat in a hospital setting, they instantly recognize this person to be a medical professional.

Not only was a white lab coat the mark of a scientist, but it was also a mark of purity. Today, doctors are trusted as people of authority, people who will treat a patient without being influenced by things like the patient's race, gender, or politics; doctors don't let personal biases get in their way.

A white lab coat was also a sign of sanitation. Doctors deal with blood and other bodily fluids. When a doctor approaches a patient in a clean white coat, the patient rarely thinks about the possibility of the doctor spreading germs from other people.

FUN FACTS

About 72% of doctors wear a lab coat at least 75% of the time.

Surgeons were the first group of doctors to wear white lab coats.

Approximately 97% of medical schools have at least one white coat ceremony in which the future doctor is presented a white lab coat; many have two, one at the beginning of the student's journey and one at graduation.

Studies have found that people are more likely to trust doctors in a white coat and business attire than a doctor wearing a white coat and something else or wearing just business attire.

Survey data reveals that patients don't expect doctors to wear the white jacket into the operating room or the emergency room; in those settings, they expect the doctors to wear scrubs.

WHY DO MANY POLICE CARS HAVE A RED LIGHT ABOVE THE POLICE OFFICER DRIVING AND A BLUE LIGHT ABOVE THE OFFICER'S PARTNER?

Have you ever been riding in a vehicle with someone when a police car pulls behind them and begins to follow them? Even the best of drivers tends to get nervous when they suspect they are being closely monitored. It gets even more nerve-wracking for the driver if the police officer turns on the lights on top of the police car. In the United States, people tend to salute the colors red, white, and blue, but, when beamed from a police car, these colors strike fear and paranoia into most drivers' hearts.

Have you ever wondered why, out of all the color combinations available, law enforcement and other emergency preparedness vehicles such as ambulances, use red and blue lights? This, of course, has not always been the case. At one time, police cars had one color of light – red, and it didn't flash. Although when combined with a siren, people could hear and see the car from a distance, emergency workers soon realized that flashing got people's attention better than a solid red light, so flashing lights – either beacons or light bars – became the standard.

Emergency workers stuck with red, though, for better reasons than just tradition. Red can be seen farther than any other color during the day. Also, red is associated with blood and life, so red readily communicates that lives are at stake. If a police car today has only its red lights flashing, the officer is on the way to a life-threatening crisis, and every second counts. Besides alerting drivers that the police officer is coming, the flashing red light also enhances the police officer's vision.

Since red is the color that can be seen farthest away during the day, it likely won't surprise you to learn that blue is the color the human eye sees best at night. Blue typically has a calming effect on people, and therefore blue is used for traveling to lesser emergencies or when the police cars have arrived at the scene. In some cases, both the blue lights and the red lights are used simultaneously when driving to an emergency, because the redlight may be mistaken by drivers to be a vehicle's brake light.

Although red and blue are the primary colors of police cars in the United States, different states, counties, and towns may also have a cream or white light that will flash intermittently with the blue. Other countries have different color codes; for instance, in England, the police generally only have blue lights on their cars. The colors of the lights and the ways of using lights vary from place to place, so, if you visit out of the country, be sure to learn the local way of doing things.

Tow trucks, utility vehicles, and other vehicles that go to the scenes of accidents but don't deal directly with human lives usually have a yellow amber light on them.

Although it is legal for people to mount light bars onto their vehicles, be sure to check with local officials before using them, for many communities in the U.S. have strict rules about using them.

Because many people are colorblind or partially colorblind and cannot see red, some countries have green and blue police lights.

Police officers often use their emergency lights in non-emergency situations – no, I'm not talking about going to the doughnut shop. For instance, police will use their emergency lights when leading a parade, when escorting prisoners, or when directing traffic at a busy intersection.

Since 2010, police have used LED (light emitting diodes) lights.

If you didn't have a smartphone and were to drive to a town you had never been to before and wanted to attend a Christian worship service, how would you find a building that housed worshippers? Many people would look for a steeple. The steeple is a distinguishing mark of many churches and is found in numerous denominations and sects.

Believe it or not, that is exactly the reason many churches are built with steeples today; the steeple makes the building easy to identify as a house of worship. Although steeples are synonymous with churches today, the modern steeple did not emerge until the 1700s. Ever since the early days worshippers have tried to reach up to the gods through architecture – remember the Tower of Babble, the pointed pyramids of ancient Egypt, and the ziggurats of ancient Babylon, and the early churches often had towers that reached skyward. These church towers typically contained a chapel and a baptistry and were part of the congregation's campus. The steeple was a new way to accomplish an old purpose.

Churches turned to steeples because they served practical purposes. Most steeples have multiple parts and therefore multiple uses; depending on how lavish it is, a steeple may have a clock, a bell tower, a spire, and then a cross or similar icon on its tip. For many towns, the church was the central focus for both spiritual and civic life; the clock was the community clock. The bell, meanwhile, was a way to communicate with the community; it was rung to call people to worship and at specific times of the day to remind people to pray. Having the bell in the steeple allowed the bell's sound to carry much farther than it would have carried if the bell was positioned at eye-level where buildings and trees could muffle the sound.

Bells were first placed on the tower, but soon the structure that housed the bell was placed on the church roof. Superstition played a part in placing these steeples on church roofs. Worshippers did not want evil spirits to enter the building, and, while the bell produced noise evil spirits were believed to find obnoxious, the design of the steeple itself was believed to prohibit spirits from approaching the church building – it had a prickly point that could impale them and steep surfaces on which they could lose their balance. Many churches even added gargoyles to the architecture to try to scare away evil beings. Although the fear of evil spirits may not be a reason modern churches continue to have steeples, the spiritual and practical reasons discussed above certainly are.

FUN FACTS

Many Anglican, Catholic, and Lutheran churches ring their bells three times per day to summon people to pray – at 6 a.m., noon, and 6 p.m.

Steeples are traditionally white. This is because most early steeples were made of wood, and wood had to be whitewashed to protect it from the weather and insect damage.

Ulm Minister, a church in Germany, is the tallest church in the world; it has a steeple that stands 515 feet (161.63 meters).

Early settlers used the church steeple as a lookout tower to see if any danger was on the horizon.

A church steeple played a major role in the American Revolution. On April 18, 1775, Robert Newton hung two lanterns in the Old North Church, Episcopal Church, in Boston to alert Paul Revere and others that the British were coming by water. Paul then made his famous midnight ride, alerting the residents the soldiers were approaching.

WHY DO RAILROAD TRACKS OFTEN HAVE GRAVEL UNDER THEM?

Did you realize that the steel rails on a railroad expand as they get warm and contract when they get cool? One would think that this would lead to the rails buckling when they expanded and to the rails contracting - breaking into pieces - when they got cold. Thanks to those cross ties – sleepers, as they say in the United Kingdom – though, that is not the case. The rails are nailed to the cross ties, and the cross ties keep the rails equal distance apart while allowing the rails to expand and contract. The crossties themselves are held in place by gravel. The gravel interlocks and gives the crossties the freedom to move while also providing a solid foundation.

The gravel, known in the industry as "ballast", is placed under, around, and on top of the crossties. Not only does it support the crossties as the rails expand and contract; it also supports the locomotives and freight cars that roll over it. (Did you realize that a typical loaded freight car weighs 130 tons and the typical locomotive weighs between 100 and 225 tons? That's a lot of weight to support!)

Not only does the gravel support the ties, but it also drains the rainwater. Whereas rainwater would collect on normal ground, it simply runs through the rocks and away from the tracks.

Meanwhile, vegetation cannot thrive in the rocky environment. This means that because of the gravel, tree roots that could cause the rails to buckle cannot take root.

The type of rock used for the railbed depends on what is available locally. For instance, an area that has lots of granite will likely use granite ballast. Ballast is a large expense, and to save money, lesser used tracks of the same line may have a ballast of coal or sand rather than granite. Also, many railroads use layers of different substances for their roadbeds. For instance, one might start with small ballast to create a solid foundation, add a layer of rubber to reduce vibration, and then add the big ballast stones to hold the crossties. The size of the ballast and how much ballast depends on the gauge of the railroad, how many trains utilize it, and what the weight of the trains is.

FUN FACTS

A mile of railroad track contains 3,249 ties.

Wooden railroad ties are typically made from hardwood, such as oak or hickory.

Different cultures have different words for railroad ties; in the United States, they are "cross ties", in the United Kingdom they are "sleepers", and in France they are "traverses".

In some places, ballast is replaced with asphalt or concrete. Although concrete requires less upkeep, its start-up cost is much higher.

The modern railroad can trace its roots to around 100 BCE when mine carts were pushed along precut grooves.

WHY ARE BEDROOMS TYPICALLY ON THE SECOND FLOOR OF A TWO-STORY HOUSE?

If you plan to serenade a girl by singing outside her window, you will likely want to bring a long pole along with you to tap on her window to get her attention – if she lives in a two-story house, her bedroom window is not likely to be on the first floor.

Ever since the introduction of the multi-story home, bedrooms have been placed on the second floor. In the day before alarm clocks were common, a person was paid to tap on windows with a pole to wake up sleeping residents, so they did not miss their shift at the factory. Although the job occupation of "knocker" is not common today, the concept of the bedrooms being on the second floor continues to be a Western tradition.

Bedrooms being on the second floor likely began as a matter of safety. In the Middle Ages, homes could not be locked securely, so the reality of a bear or wolf entering was a real concern. By being upstairs, the family was much safer from predators.

When better locks were invented, people continued to still keep the bedrooms on the second floor. At that time, each floor of the two-story home was treated as a distinct entity. The first floor was the public floor, and upstairs was the private residence. The household's guests dined and were entertained on the first floor; the second floor was the family's private space and was off limits to the guests.

Today, the downstairs rooms tend to be the rooms utilized during the day and the upstairs rooms are the rooms utilized at night. Most people who live in a two-story house get dressed in their bedroom and then come downstairs to eat and socialize. Throughout the day, the bedrooms receive little use while both family and friends use the living room, game room, kitchen, and dining room downstairs. Enjoying these activities downstairs makes sense – climbing stairs takes time, can be noisy, and is a hindrance in many cases. Also, refrigerators and stoves are extremely heavy, so it makes sense to keep the equipment and activities associated with them on the lower level.

A fourth reason is also practical – heat rises and having the bedrooms on the second-floor captures used heat. The kitchen produces heat from cooking and the living room from warm bodies, and this heat travels upstairs. Even the fireplace heat which warmed the living room seeps upstairs.

The centuries-old fad of having the bedroom on the second floor is gradually changing. Because many people want to show off mountain views or beach views to their friends, they are building "upside down houses", homes with bedrooms on the first floor. These homeowners want to entertain guests upstairs so they can show off the view. The change, though, is very gradual, and the majority of bedrooms will be on the second floor for the foreseeable future.

FUN FACTS

A two-story home is 15-20% cheaper to build than if the same rooms were built on one level.

Some cities and home-owner associations have laws dictating if trees can be/must be near bedroom windows.

To prevent falls, elderly people are encouraged to live in single floor ranch homes.

Upside-down houses are common in Scandinavian countries.

Bedrooms on the second floor are typically more private from passersby and road traffic than bedrooms on the first floor.

PART 5

TRADITIONS IN WESTERN SOCIETY

Pause reading for a minute, grab three sheets of paper and some tape. Place the papers side by side and tape them together by putting tape on the upper left-hand corner and the upper right-hand corner of the centerpiece; do the same with the lower left and lower right corners. Now, lift the line of paper and look carefully at the seams where the papers meet. Do you see a gap?

Ancient people believed that the universe was on a timeline, just like those papers formed a line. They also believed that a gap existed between the seam where one year met another year, and that evil spirits from the other side could get into our world from the spirit world through the gap at that time.

Believing that evil spirits did not like to be around noisy places, people made as much noise as possible at the moment that it was most likely the evil spirits would come – the stroke of midnight, the exact moment one year transferred to another. Although most people today don't know why they do it, they continue the tradition of blowing noisemakers, loudly wishing each other, "Happy New Year!", and listening to fireworks. Just as the ancients used to hug loved ones to celebrate that they had overcome the danger, we turn to our loved one and give that person a hug and a kiss.

Today, the "evil spirits" have been downgraded to "ill will" and "bad luck"; you will hear people proclaim that blowing noise makers keeps bad luck away. Another luck-bringing New Year superstition and/or tradition includes eating black-eyed peas. Not only do the peas supposedly bring one luck but also riches.

The ancient Celts didn't celebrate New Year's Day on January 1 as we do; they began the year on November 1. We – unknowingly to most people – continue this ancient New Year's tradition of evil spirits slipping through the crack of time by dressing up as scary creatures. The ancients called the day New Year's Eve; we call it Halloween, hallowed eve.

Not only did the ancients believe there was a gap in time between the completion of one crop cycle to the next, they also believed that each person also had a full cycle of days and that a gap between the spirit world and our world was possible at that time as well. They claimed the cycle began on the date one was born, and therefore one was at risk from an attack from the spirit world any time one had a birthday. Therefore, friends and family gathered near the birthday person to sing loudly, play boisterous games, and have rowdy feasts to keep the birthday person safe. We continue this tradition through modern birthday parties, where we sing the birthday song, play games, and eat cake.

FUN FACTS

New Year's Day and birthdays were not celebrated until after the calendar was invented; the calendar was invented 11,000 years ago.

The root of the word "calendar" means "to call out"; the calendar announced the new moon.

Although not all countries use the Gregorian calendar and therefore do not celebrate the New Year on January 1, New Year's Day is the holiday shared by more countries than any other holiday.

The Roman new year began on the day public officials were sworn into office to begin their duties. In 45 B.C., when the modern calendar began, this happened to be January 1, and therefore January 1 was declared to be the first month of the year.

England and its colonies, which included the United States, did not officially adopt January 1 as the start of the new year until 1752.

Society is full of rules. Some are written into legislation. For instance, on the highways of the United States there are speed limits posted, and if you exceed the posted speed and get caught, you end up with a traffic ticket and possible jail time. Other rules, though, are not written into the law books but are still expected to be followed. One of these unwritten rules in the United States is not to wear white after Labor Day, which is always celebrated on the first Monday in September. (Other cultures also have end-of-the-summer holidays but they call their holiday a Banker's holiday; for instance, in England the last Monday in August is always a Banker's Holiday; it is a day to celebrate absolutely nothing, just to enjoy life.)

Some people claim that the rule is merely a way to mark the change in the seasons. White clothing reflects the sun's rays and keeps one cooler than dark clothing, and therefore with winter coming on and people wanting to retain warmth,

Labor Day marks the time to bring out the dark-colored sweaters. For children of yesteryear who didn't have year-round schooling, Labor Day was a time to turn in the white t-shirts of summer and put on something both warmer and dressier as they returned to school.

Perhaps the idea that white shouldn't be worn after Labor Day has been ingrained in Western culture from the beginning, but it only became a spoken rule in the 1800s. In the 1800s, the wealthy – the people with an astounding amount of leisure time and/or the people who made business decisions, wore white year-round. In fact, even today you may hear an office worker called a white-collar worker because that person typically works with the brain instead of the brawn. Wearing white was a subtle way of telling everyone that you were so rich that you didn't have to get your hands or clothes dirty.

In the 1800s, two types of wealthy people existed in the United States – the people who were well-established in wealth and those who still had to work part of the year to be able to generate wealth to keep up with the former. Both groups went to the seashore in the summer and could be seen in white tennis outfits at the local country club. However, the latter had to trade in their white tennis outfits for business suits nine months of the year. The city was a dirty place, and clothes quickly became soiled – if you don't believe me, look at a picture of city life from the 1880s to the 1930s, and you will notice that everyone is wearing dark clothing; the dark clothing was a way to hide the grime. For the newly rich, the rule of wearing white in the summer at their retreat but not during the other months when they worked in the city was both a means of comfort and a way to distinguish themselves from the lower class.

Society has moved beyond the Gilded Age, but the rule of not wearing white after Labor Day is still around. Some people, such as my mother, believe in following it, but if someone wears white after Labor Day, it is no longer a social faux pas. Just as wearing socks with sandals does not make one an outcast, wearing white after Labor Day may get you some strange looks and perhaps a few comments, but you are not going to be shunned for doing so.

FUN FACTS

Labor Day was declared a national holiday in the United States by President Grover Cleveland in 1894; the purpose of the day is to celebrate the American worker.

Many other countries celebrate a holiday honoring the work force too, often calling it International Workers Day; the most popular date for the celebration is May 1.

Today's fashion experts recommend going by the weight of a fabric instead of the color when deciding if it is appropriate to wear.

For decades, "summer" in the American mind began on Memorial Day, the last Monday in May, and ended on Labor Day, the first Monday in September.

Around the 1900s the upper class in the United States had very specific rules about how to dress. Although lots of people were getting rich and trying to prove they were upper class by spending money, only the true upper class knew all the social codes.

WHY DO WE GO DOOR-TO-DOOR COLLECTING CANDY ON HALLOWEEN?

I don't know about your parents, but my parents have some rules that contradict each other. For instance, 364 days of the year they tell me, "Don't talk to strangers" and "Don't take candy from strangers" but every Halloween night they insist that I go door-to-door so total strangers can toss candy into the bag I was carrying. (I will admit that they did watch from the street while I went to the door and that perhaps – but I have my doubts – they knew everybody that they had me approach.)

The ritual of knocking on doors Halloween night is commonly called trick-or-treating. On Halloween, adults as well as children put on scary costumes, making themselves into witches and ghosts in preparation for going door to door. Non-scary costumed people, such as those wearing pop culture characters like Scooby Doo and Superman, can also be seen going door to door. Although almost everyone takes the candy-begging ritual light-heartedly, the children are actually using extortion, claiming that if the household does not give them a treat, then they will come back and do a mischievous trick.

Although trick-or-treating has become a light-hearted time for today's children, it has roots going back over 3,000 years – and the traditions it combines were taken very seriously in those days. The Celtic culture - which later became the French, German, and English cultures - believed that October 31 was the last day of fall as well as the last day of the year. They knew that when two things overlap, they don't always have a perfect seal, and, since the years were overlapping, the Celts believed the dead could enter this world on Halloween. Fortunately, most of the dead just wanted to visit, and so the dead came through the opening and then returned to the opening before it closed. To welcome the dead – or to try to make peace with the dead, people would set out food for the dead. In fact, they sometimes set out a full meal, and, believe it or not, it was eaten. (Woodland critters may have had something to do with this, but the Celtics firmly believed the missing food was evidence the spirit had visited. To keep the house safe, residents set out whatever they thought the spirit wanted; if the spirit wanted sweets, the spirit got sweets. Therefore, to this day, people set out candy, which is exactly what the scary creatures approaching their homes want.

People believed if they went out onto the streets, the spirits might hurt them. Most people stayed home locked in their dwelling, but the bravest disguised themselves as spirits and went wherever they had to go. That's right, we do just as they did; we put on a costume if we go out on Halloween.

By the 1600s the belief that the dead returned to eat on Halloween had begun to fade; the traditions continued, but with new twists. On Halloween children in Scotland would go "guising", going door to door to sing or recite a poem and then ask for a donation. Doing a trick, such as reciting a poem, would lead to a treat. Instead of saying "trick or treat", though, they would say, "Help the Halloween party." The idea of going door to door to collect for a Halloween party caught on in other countries. Although immigrants brought Halloween to the United States, the Puritans who first settled in New England did not welcome it.

The phrase "Trick or treat" was first heard in Canada in 1917 and variations, such as "Tricks or treats" and "trick or a treat" worked their way quickly into the United States. By the 1940s, today's trick-or-treat ritual of children going door to door and saying, "Trick or treat" and then receiving candy was in place in the United States. In other cultures, though, the modern ritual was much later; Scottish children just began saying "trick or treat" in the 2000s.

FUN FACTS

"Halloween" means "hallowed evening".

The Celts didn't call Halloween "Halloween"; they called their New Year's Eve holiday "Samhain". On Samhain, they had roaring bonfires and made sacrifices to the dead.

Some people who celebrated Samhain dressed up as ghosts and evil spirits to try to intimidate other ghosts.

When Christianity replaced the Celts, Samhain became All Soul's Day, a time for honoring the dead with bonfires and masquerading.

During World War II, children in the United States still went trick-or-treating, but they gathered very little candy because of sugar rationing.

When you stop and think about it, Americans are very complex. One day they are thankful for everything they have and then literally the next day they are shopping for more, more, and more.

Although the public did not refer to the post-Thanksgiving holiday sales – the kickoff of the Christmas shopping season – as Black Friday until recently, the name was actually created in Philadelphia in the 1950s and spread from there. Many factory workers wanted a four-day weekend but were required to come to work on the Friday after Thanksgiving. Although they were required to be at work, many came down with "Thanksgiving-itus" and missed work that Friday. Possibly with thoughts of the Black Plague in mind, Philadelphia factory bosses described this annual plague as Black Friday.

Philadelphia may be nicknamed "the city of brotherly love", but the local police found no love lost among shoppers competing for scarce gifts. Not only were the citizens of the community participating in the shopping ritual, so were numerous people who came from the suburbs. The shoppers eagerly looked forward to the shopping day; children eagerly looked forward to being out of school and to the arrival of Santa; and the police dreaded the day and referred to it as "Black Friday", meaning that it was a time of sadness and difficulty for them – crowd control issues, traffic issues, shoplifting issues; pickpocketing and petty crimes; and traffic accidents.

Merchants overheard the police talking, and worried that the public was going to overhear the police as well. Until this time, the public had always referred to the sales as the post-Thanksgiving sale, but now merchants wanted them to call it Big Friday, as in the biggest Friday of the year.

Merely billing the day as Big Friday did not stop the police in Philadelphia and other places from calling it Black Friday. Deciding that they couldn't stop the use of the negative term "Black Friday", the merchants decided to put a positive spin on it. They began to claim that Black Friday was the start of their most profitable time of the year – which was indeed true for many. Whereas red ink meant going into debt, black ink meant a profit, so the term Black Friday was promoted to mean keeping merchants in business.

In the late teens of the twenty-first century, businesses began trying to get other businesses' clientele by opening early on Black Friday. Within a couple of years, the stores were literally starting "Black Friday" on Thanksgiving afternoon. The following year, other businesses countered by starting "Black Friday Sales" in early November. Whereas in 2018 people would literally line up for blocks to get into stores, by 2023, only a few traditionalists actually stood in line outside store doors. In their greed, the merchants appear to have diluted the chaos associated with Black Friday, making it just another shopping day.

When Black Friday became popular, it primarily benefited downtown city merchants. Other groups saw potential in marketing around Black Friday, and numerous spinoffs by special interests were spawned. Today, Black Friday, which is focused on the malls and chain stores, is followed by Small Business Saturday, which focuses on mom-and-pop stores; Cyber Monday, which focuses on online shopping; and Charity Tuesday, which focuses on giving to others.

FUN FACTS

The first time the term "Black Friday" was used, it referred to a gold market crash in 1869. (That incident is totally unrelated to how the shopping day after Thanksgiving received its name.)

Black Friday is NOT the most profitable day of the year for most stores; the Saturday before Christmas has that honor.

The earliest recorded instance of the day after Thanksgiving being referred to as Black Friday comes from 1951.

College football also led to the term Black Friday. The Army-Navy game is always played the Saturday after Thanksgiving; therefore, not only did the police have holiday shoppers to contend with on Black Friday and Black Saturday, but they also had rowdy fans and game traffic.

Black Friday promotions include sale discounts, doorbusters, promotional bundles, coupons for one's next visit, and numerous other marketing gimmicks.

Go to any professional sporting event in the United States – football, soccer, hockey, basketball, auto racing - and you will likely be asked to stand for the national anthem right before the start of the game. In fact, the national anthem is such a part of baseball that many people are under the illusion that it concludes with the words, "Play ball!"

It hasn't always been this way, though. In fact, the United States did not even have a national anthem until 1931. Although Francis Scott Key had written *The Star Spangled Banner*, originally titled *D'fense* of Fort McHenry, on April 14, 1814, following the British bombardment of Fort McHenry in Baltimore during the War of 1812, it did not become the national anthem until Congress passed and President Herbert Hoover signed a measure designating it as such.

Although it was not the official national anthem until 1931, *The Star Spangled Banner* had been played in ballparks prior to then. The first time was May 15, 1862, in Brooklyn, New York at the opening of the Union Baseball and Cricket Grounds. The song became associated with baseball on September 5, 1918, when it was played prior to the first game of the World Series. World War I was raging, and baseball players wanted to show their support to the soldiers on the front lines; in fact, league officials had thought of canceling the series but the soldiers themselves welcomed it as a diversion and asked that it continue. Whereas today the national anthem is played at the beginning of the game, on that memorable day in 1918 it was sung during the seventh inning stretch. The Red Sox beat the Cubs 1-0 in an intense pitcher's duel that September day, but the next day the newspapers focused on the anthem more than the game.

Hiring a band to play, though, was an expense, so the anthem was played only on special occasions until the 1940s when World War II broke out. During World War II, American patriotism was high again, and Americans wanted to show the troops that they supported them; one way of showing this support was to show a whole stadium on its feet standing at attention singing the national anthem before the baseball game began. By this time, both recorded music and quality sound systems were available, so stadiums began blaring the music for people to sing to. Although the anthem was first associated with baseball, other events quickly adopted it as well, and a trip to the ballpark meant an opportunity to unite one's voice with others in respect for the troops. Not everyone at the stadium was in favor of the war, of course, but those who did not respect the troops were still encouraged to participate since the flag also represented the country, the concepts of freedom, liberty, and self-expression.

After the war ended, a public consensus was reached that one should not only show one's patriotism during war but also in times of peace. As noted above, the flag represented much more than just the troops; it was a symbol that all

Americans, regardless of how they divided themselves by race, gender, or team preference, could relate to.

In recent days, some athletes have chosen to kneel instead of stand during the national anthem to protest police brutality, to raise their fists to protest racial inequality, or to simply go about getting ready for the game as the anthem is played. Most commissioners and coaches are embarrassed about the behavior and do not agree with the players that the singing of the national anthem should be a time for political statements. Whether the anthem continues to be a part of sports remains to be seen.

FUN FACTS

Although people were aware of T*he Star Spangled Banner* prior to the Civil War, they preferred the songs *Yankee Doodle* and *Hail Columbia* to be the national anthem should the United States adopt one.

John Stafford Smith set Francis Scott Key's *The Star Spangled Banner* poem to the tune of the popular British drinking song to which it is sung today.

The Star Spangled Banner has four verses, but only the first verse is sung at the ballparks.

Whereas states tended to perceive themselves as independent entities prior to the Civil War, after the Civil War the federal government became the dominant power and the flag, the star-spangled banner, became a unifying symbol.

In the National Football League (NFL) players who do not want to stand at attention to the national anthem do not have to do so; but they are asked to wait in the locker-room until it has finished playing.

When you say your prayers at night, do you kneel and use the bed as an altar? Do you have a prayer mat, and lay your body flat upon it? We kneel and lay flat as a sign of reverence for the Divine; we kneel to show that the Divine, not us, has all the power. We kneel in awe, reverence, and respect.

Showing reverence for the Divine has been a part of human worship from the earliest days of religion. People wanted to appease the gods and win the gods' favor, and so they humbled themselves before the gods. When the concept of king arose in human society, people treated the king much like they treated their gods; they showed the king reverence by bowing down to him.

By the Middle Ages, the king surrounded himself with family and friends; this inner circle was known as the king's court. To be a member of the king's court was something most middle-class people longed to become. Needless to say, some of the people at court were single women. Men, who were accustomed to bowing to the God and king they revered, began to bow to the maidens as well. When it was appropriate to ask the maiden for her hand in marriage, the knight humbled himself by getting on one knee.

A recent survey shows that 85% of men have proposed on bended knee. Most don't realize the custom dates back to the earliest years of humankind; they just know it is a tradition that they want to carry on. Exactly how the one-one knee pose looks varies, and there is no set rule regarding which knee that one must get on; one etiquette book may suggest the right knee but another etiquette book will suggest the left. Most people agree that the man should be able to get up quickly in case his maiden flees, and that generally means being on one's dominant knee; in other words, if you are right-handed you will likely get on your right knee.

Although the custom of proposing on bended knee remains common, that is certainly not the only way to propose. Also, today, women are free to propose as well. As you get to know the other person, you will come to realize what they expect a proposal to look like; everybody is different, so don't assume anything. Remember, the goal is to show that you love, respect, and revere the other person, so choose something that causes them to feel those feelings.

FUN FACTS

The concept of "courting" refers to the romantic traditions of the king's court.

Knights not only kneeled when proposing marriage to a maiden, the knight often kneeled to swear allegiance and servitude to various married women of the court as well.

People who are knighted by the English king are expected to kneel in respect; the king will then knight them by touching a sword to their back.

The fancy term for proposing on one knee is called "genuflecting"; the word is based on the Latin words for "bended knee".

Getting on one-knee is not the only courtly tradition still found in our culture. Another is the male asking the girl's parents for permission to marry her before popping the question to her.

WHY DO WE TURN OUR CLOCKS AHEAD IN THE SPRING AND TURN THEM BACK IN THE FALL?

Traditions come and go. Most countries in Asia, South America, Australia, and Central America once had a tradition of setting their clocks ahead an hour for part of the year, but, with a couple of exceptions, they no longer have it. In the United States, and Europe, though, the practice of Daylight Savings Time (DST) is still an annual event. Have you ever wondered who came up with the idea, why they came up with it, and why the time shifts happen at 2 a.m.?

Benjamin Franklin, an American inventor and politician, proposed the idea of Daylight Savings Time for the United States in 1784. Daylight Savings Time would move one hour of daylight from the morning into the evening; he believed the extra hour of daylight would be beneficial to the farmers. The idea of Daylight Savings Time was implemented during World War I in France, Germany, Great Britain, and the United States; the extra hour of daylight meant energy savings, such as not having to turn on lights for the hour.

The idea was utilized again in the United States during World

War II – people called it "war time" – and the tradition became a yearly routine in 1966. Many people, such as factory workers, liked the extra hour of sunlight to go outside after work, and businesses liked it because people were more inclined to leave their homes to shop. Ironically, farmers didn't like it, believing it clogged the roads when they needed to haul crops to the market. Also, researchers have determined that it doesn't save that much energy. The real beneficiaries and losers have been economic interests – department stores enjoy the extra hour of customers while movie theaters and other evening attractions despise it. The future of Daylight Savings Time is uncertain.

One of the weirdest things about Daylight Savings Time is that it always begins and ends at 2 a.m. If you're like me, you're probably wondering who is likely to be up at 2 a.m. to see this time change. That, though, is exactly the point – 2 a.m. was chosen because 2 a.m. is the hour the fewest trains were running, and therefore that's when the fewest people would be inconvenienced or confused.

FUN FACTS

In the European Union, Daylight Savings Time begins on the last Sunday in March and ends on the last Sunday in October. In the United States, it lasts a little longer, beginning on the second Sunday of March and ending on the first Sunday of November.

Many towns around the world had an annual program of Daylight Savings Time changes many years before any nation required them to do it.

Germany-Austria was the first nation to adopt Daylight Savings Time; it started on April 30, 1916.

Although the United States officially has Daylight Savings Time, states can opt out completely, such as Hawaii and Arizona have done, or give their individual communities a choice, such as Indiana has done.

Finding the extra hour of daylight is thought to be very emotionally healthy; however, the health benefits must be weighed against the fact that one's physical body must adjust to the hour change.

WHY DO WE SAY "CHEESE" AS A PICTURE IS BEING TAKEN?

What does cheese have to do with photography?

If you go to a professional photographer, you are likely going to be asked to say, "Cheese" immediately before the picture is snapped. We can thank U.S. President Franklin Delano Roosevelt for this tradition.

Image is important to politicians, and Franklin Delano Roosevelt wanted to come across as a positive, upbeat person. He guided the United States through the Great Depression and World War II, and he believed Americans needed a leader who could see happy days ahead. These were troubling times, and he wanted to project hope and happiness even though there was a lot to justify feeling hopeless. Just like all of us, he had moments when he did not feel happy, but he knew how to make himself smile for the cameras and still project that positive image– he would say the word "cheese". Whether he discovered the secret of putting on a smile or if someone told him, he is credited with sharing the idea with Joseph E. Davies, a U.S. ambassador who shared the idea with the world.

Pause for a minute and say the word, "Cheese". Now, focus on the "ch" sound. Notice how your lips move vertically. Now pronounce the "eee" sound. Again, notice how your lips move; this time they are moving horizontally. The word "cheese" tends to put a smile on your face, and, as if pronouncing it does not, just saying something silly is enough to bring out the smile in many people.

Believe it or not, prior to the 1900s, people did not smile for pictures. In the Victorian era, it was considered a social faux pas to smile for a picture. At that time, a small mouth was thought to be beautiful. Also, most people had missing teeth, and the teeth they had needed major dental work, so the mouth was nothing to be proud of. Photography was expensive from 1826-1900, and since people generally got their pictures taken only once in a lifetime, they did not want to be caught in faux pas – looking like a drunk or a child – on camera.

Smiling on camera, though, became commonplace around 1900. That year, Kodak came out with the Brownie camera; the camera was priced so the middle class could afford it, and it was easy enough to operate so that the common person could take photographs. This meant that one's picture was often taken in casual moments, moments when one was smiling.

A smile is an innate nonverbal gesture representing happiness; it doesn't matter what culture one goes to, if someone is happy, they will smile. Just as politicians like Franklin Roosevelt wanted to project the image of happiness, so did those being photographed, and smiling for the camera became the new trend.

FUN FACTS

The first photograph, "View from the Window at Le Gras" was taken by Joseph Niepce, a French inventor, in 1826.

Over 2000 varieties of cheese exist.

Saying "cheese" will make you smile; eating cheese right before bed will help you sleep. Cheese has calcium in it which stimulates the body's melatonin which causes sleep.

Digital photography became commonplace in 1995 when digital cameras were released to the public by Casio and Kodak. Prior to then, most people had to take photographs and then mail them to a lab to have the film developed.

To keep people's mouths small in pictures prior to 1900, photographers instructed people to, "Say prunes."

WHY DO MANY PEOPLE BELIEVE THIRTEEN IS AN UNLUCKY NUMBER?

Do you suffer from paraskeviekatriaphobia?

Paraskevidekatriaphobia is the fear of Friday the Thirteenth. While over ten percent of the population of the United States has a fear of the number thirteen, even more have a specific fear of Friday the Thirteenth. To accommodate these fears, multi-floored buildings often avoid having a thirteenth floor open to the public, the number 13 is not assigned to wear on an athletic jersey, no gate is dubbed Gate 13 at the airport terminal, hotels don't assign a room number 13, merchants round up change to fifteen cents rather than handing somebody thirteen cents, and bosses let employees use time-off on Friday the Thirteenth.

The fear of thirteen is an ancient fear; it is definitely not something recent. Some claim the fear can be seen back as far as human writing goes; for instance, the first legal document, the Code of Hammurabi written in 1730 B.C.E., left out rule thirteen, skipping from twelve to fourteen. (People who don't believe the ancients were superstitious simply claim the scribe who translated the work made a clerical error.)

What is so bad about the number 13? To begin with, thirteen had a bad reputation because it wasn't twelve. The ancients had a fascination with twelve. A day consisted of two sets of 12 hours. A year consisted of 12 months. In Jewish culture, there were Twelve Tribes of Israel. Thirteen was considered evil because thirteen items looked so close to twelve, but they weren't twelve. Because of its ability to fool, 13 became regarded as the worst number of all.

Als, thirteen was a copy-cat number, a "compound number". That is, instead of having its own name as numbers 1-12 had, thirteen blended the names "3" and the "10", creating three-teen.

The fact that Judas Iscariot was the thirteenth guest at the Last Supper in the Bible didn't help 13's cause; similarly, in Norse mythology, Loki, the thirteenth guest at the god's banquet, was the one who introduced chaos into the world.

Many bad things have happened in history on Friday the Thirteenth. For instance, on October 13, 1507, Phillip IV of France arrested and eventually killed all the Knights of Templar. Most people have friends and family who can testify of bad things that have happened on Friday the Thirteenth. These events are history and cannot be denied. Although one's logical side states that these terrible occurrences are just coincidence, most people are hesitant to do anything risky - to invest in stocks, get an operation, or get married. In more extreme cases, people are hesitant to even go to work, or, get this, to get out of bed. Most people admit that it may be purely coincidence that something bad happening to their friend or relative on Friday the Thirteenth was merely coincidence, but most people also reason that there is no need to take a chance.

FUN FACTS

A given year can have three Friday the Thirteenths; it is also possible to go fourteen months without a Friday the Thirteenth.

In China, the numeral 4 is pronounced like "death", and therefore Chinese and many Asian cultures avoid using the numeral 4 just as Americans avoid the numeral 13.

Ancient Egypt considered 13 to be a lucky number.

Fear of the number 13 is called triskaidekaphobia.

Editors often follow the principle of spelling out numbers 1-12 and then using numerals for numbers 13 and above.

WHY DO CHILDREN HIDE TEETH UNDER THEIR PILLOW FOR THE TOOTH FAIRY?

On the surface, the answer to the question of "why do children hide teeth under their pillow for the Tooth Fairy" is obvious – to get money. The Tooth Fairy will generally exchange the tooth for money. The amount of money a child receives will vary based on the family's economic status, whether it is a special tooth such as the first one or the last one, and how hard it was to remove. This, though, raises questions, such as "why is the tooth fairy willing to give money for the tooth?" and "what becomes of all of those baby teeth?"

Teeth begin to come in when a child is three months old. However, when a child is around six years old, one's mouth has grown and one's baby teeth will be beginning to be pushed out of the way by one's adult teeth. In the ideal situation, the new tooth grows under the baby tooth; it will cause the tooth to dissolve and push the tooth out. Losing one's baby teeth is natural, and something all healthy people do.

The Legend of the Tooth Fairy began to appear in Norse mythology around 1300. Believe it or not, the Tooth Fairy was not the only person willing to pay children for a baby tooth. Soldiers, including Viking warriors, were willing to pay; they believed that if they wore a necklace of baby teeth, they would have good luck in battle. One's enemies, especially witches, were willing to pay as well; they wanted to have a piece of one's child to curse the child or the family. To ensure that their children did not give the lost tooth to soldiers, witches, or those who collected on their behalf, parents told children that the tooth fairy would come and give them a better deal; this inspired the children to bring the lost tooth safely home.

Walt Disney unintentionally influenced the way modern children perceive the Tooth Fairy. Throughout history, the tooth fairy has been perceived primarily as a mouse or a pixie. Children in countries such as Spain, Mexico, much of South America, and China picture the tooth fairy as a mouse– don't laugh; mice grow teeth as long as they live just like you and I grow fingernails, mice are known for collecting things and putting them in their nest, and mice move very sneakily when they think no one is looking. In European and American cultures, the tooth fairy is a pixie. Unlike Santa Clause who makes rounds each December or the Easter Bunny, who is available for pictures in most American malls around Easter, no one has seen the Tooth Fairy. Almost every child in American culture has the same image of the Tooth Fairy, though, thanks to Walt Disney. Most people perceive The Tooth Fairy to be almost identical to Tinkerbell, the mischievous fairy friend of Peter Pan in the 1953 movie *Peter Pan*.

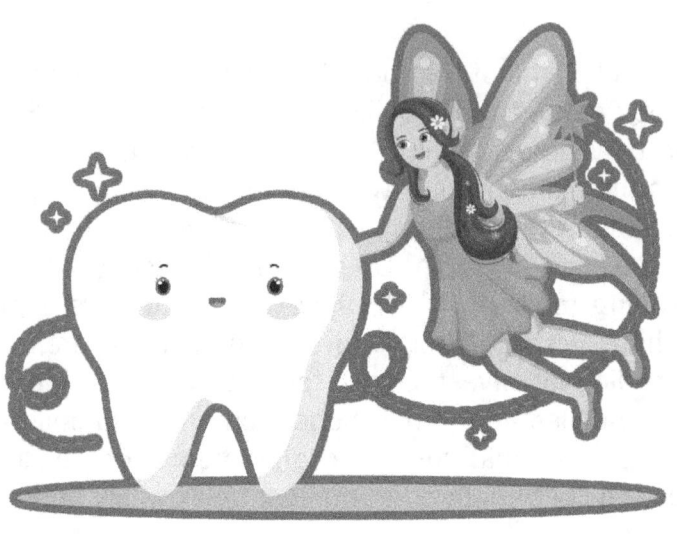

FUN FACTS

In Japan, when children lose a tooth, the child throws it either straight up or straight down. If the child loses an upper tooth in Japan, the child should throw it straight into the ground; this is supposed to help its replacement come in straight. Meanwhile, if the child loses a lower tooth, the child is to throw it as straight into the air as possible; this will help the replacement lower tooth come in straight.

In Korea, children throw their teeth onto the roof of their house. When a magpie comes for the tooth, it is thought to carry it to the gods, bringing the person good luck.

Many children find that the Tooth Fairy pays more for a tooth with no cavities than a tooth with cavities; this is done to encourage children to brush their teeth regularly.

Prior to the Tooth Fairy collecting teeth in Norse society, baby teeth were usually given a burial.

In pre-Islamic Egypt, children would throw their tooth into the air as an offering for the Sun god.

CONCLUSION

We have now looked at 50 why questions. It's time now for you to learn how to construct your own "why" question so you can keep learning. If you are going to get good answers, you must first ask good questions.

Have you ever noticed that the word "quest" exists in "question"? A good question will lead you on a learning adventure. Here are some traits of a good "why" question:

- It should be of interest to you.

- It should not be able to be answered with a simple yes or no.

- It should be very specific; there should be no vagueness about it; it will focus your research.

- It should be unbiased. For instance, you can investigate the history of an "idea" or a "custom" but not a "stupid idea" or "silly custom".

- It should not force a specific conclusion. Many times, you may have preconceived ideas about the answer, but don't word your question so that you can only explore that route. As you research you may find that you were wrong, or, in most cases, only aware of part of the answer.

- Always seek an answer from two or more sources. On the surface, the sources will not always agree, but, in many cases, the two can be meshed into an answer that contradicts none of them.

We live in a fascinating world!

Most of the time, though, most people take this world for granted. When we start to ask "why," we begin to understand that the world is very complex.

I hope you have enjoyed learning about the topics covered. More importantly, I hope that you have begun to appreciate asking questions and seeking answers. You are destined to be a lifelong learner. When your official schooling is complete and there are no more teachers, no more books, and no more principals, you will need to keep asking "why?" and seek the answers to your question. It won't matter what your profession is – teacher, business leader, farmer, plumber, computer technician, or something else – you are going to be presented with difficult problems and asked to find the answers to them. In all cases, asking good questions will lead you toward good answers.

REFERENCES

Part 1: International Customs

Question 1: Why Do They Run the Bulls in Spain?
https://www.businessinsider.com/why-people-participate-in-pamplonas-running-of-the-bulls-2015-7
https://www.cgaa.org/article/how-much-does-a-bull-weigh
https://www.healthline.com/health/how-fast-can-a-human-run#speed-comparison
https://kidadl.com/facts/animals/bull-facts
https://matadornetwork.com/trips/12-things-didnt-know-running-bulls/
https://www.mybucketlistevents.com/event-detail/pamplona-running-bulls-faqs/
https://www.runningofthebulls.com/travel/travel-tips/ready-to-run-with-bulls/
https://www.thoughtco.com/running-of-the-bulls-4766650
https://www.usatoday.com/story/news/world/2017/07/06/spain-running-bulls/455039001/
https://whatthingsweigh.com/how-much-does-a-bull-weigh/

Question 2: Why Do the English Celebrate "Guy Fawkes Night" Every November 5?
https://en.wikipedia.org/wiki/Gunpowder_Plot
https://www.britannica.com/topic/Guy-Fawkes-Day
https://en.wikipedia.org/wiki/Guy_Fawkes
https://en.wikipedia.org/wiki/Guy_Fawkes_Night
https://www.wikihow.com/Celebrate-Guy-Fawkes-Day

Question 3: Why Do We Say "Bless You" When Someone Sneezes?
https://awesomestuff365.com/fun-facts-about-sneezing/
https://en.wikipedia.org/wiki/God_bless_you#Origins_and_legends
https://en.wikipedia.org/wiki/Response_to_sneezing
https://www.nysinuscenter.com/2016/11/fun-sneezing-facts/
https://www.rd.com/article/why-do-people-say-bless-you/
https://www.snopes.com/fact-check/bless-you/

Question 4: Why Do Bagpipe Players from Scotland Wear Skirts?
https://en.wikipedia.org/wiki/Kilt
https://kiltsshop.com/what-did-scots-wear-before-kilts/
https://kiltsshop.com/why-do-scots-wear-kilts/
https://macgregorandmacduff.co.uk/blogs/news/why-do-scots-wear-kilts
https://www.scotland.com/blog/the-scottish-kilt-a-brief-history/
https://www.ukkilt.com/why-do-scots-wear-kilts/
https://venuszine.com/why-did-the-scots-wear-kilts-instead-of-pants/

Question 5: Why Do Germans Call It "The Easter Hare" Instead of "The Easter Bunny"?
https://www.bbc.com/culture/article/20230403-the-easter-bunny-evolution-of-a-symbol
https://theconversation.com/sacred-hares-banished-winter-witches-and-pagan-worship-the-roots-of-easter-bunny-traditions-are-ancient-180484
https://en.wikipedia.org/wiki/Easter_Bunny
https://furwingsandscalythings.com/rabbit-vs-bunny-vs-hare/
https://facts.net/hare-vs-rabbit/
https://icwdm.org/species/other-mammals/hares/

https://www.msn.com/en-us/lifestyle/pets/fascinating-facts-about-bunnies-we-didn-t-know/ https://wildlifeinformer.com/types-of-hares/

Question 6: Why Is Boxing Day Celebrated in Many Countries Every December 26?
https://www.almanac.com/boxing-day
https://www.bbc.co.uk/newsround/46454700
https://www.britannica.com/topic/Boxing-Day
https://en.wikipedia.org/wiki/Boxing_Day
https://en.wikipedia.org/wiki/Twelve_Days_of_Christmas
https://inews.co.uk/news/boxing-day-why-called-meaning-name-explained-christmas-2022-bank-holiday-dates-2042554

Question 7: Why Is Figgy Pudding Popular at Christmas?
https://en.wikipedia.org/wiki/Figgy_pudding
https://genius.com/Christmas-songs-we-wish-you-a-merry-christmas-lyrics
https://www.npr.org/sections/thesalt/2015/12/20/460488236/oh-bring-us-some-wait-what-is-figgy-pudding
https://people.howstuffworks.com/culture-traditions/holidays-christmas/christmas-caroler1.htm
https://www.tasteofhome.com/article/what-the-heck-is-figgy-pudding-and-why-do-we-sing-about-it/
https://yesterdaysamerica.com/the-little-known-history-of-the-caroling-tradition/

Question 8: Why Do People Hit Pinatas?
https://www.bibleinfo.com/en/questions/what-are-seven-deadly-sins https://charmpopcards.com/pinata-fun-facts.html
https://en.wikipedia.org/wiki/Piñata
https://www.npr.org/2021/12/22/1064546215/pinata-mexico-posadas-celebration https://www.spanish.academy/blog/the-most-fascinating-facts-about-the-latin-american-pinata/

Question 9: Why Do Judges - and Lawyers - in the United Kingdom Wear White Wigs?
https://www.knowswhy.com/why-do-lawyers-in-england-wear-wigs/
https://www.law.ac.uk/resources/blog/why-do-barristers-wear-wigs/
https://www.liveabout.com/law-firm-dress-code-for-men-2164254
https://reyabogado.com/us/why-do-brits-wear-wigs-in-court/#google_vignette
https://www.urbo.com/content/this-is-why-british-lawyers-still-wear-wigs-and-robes-in-court/

Question 10: Why Do Germans Celebrate Oktoberfest?
https://www.britannica.com/topic/Oktoberfest
https://dragonsnest.de/en/germany/why-is-oktoberfest-important-to-german-culture
https://en.wikipedia.org/wiki/Oktoberfest
https://www.nationalgeographic.com/culture/article/oktoberfest-munich-tradition-history
https://www.worldatlas.com/articles/why-is-oktoberfest-celebrated.html

Question 11: Why Do We Clap to Show Appreciation?
https://www.ancientpages.com/2016/05/16/clapping-to-show-appreciation-is-an-ancient-and-widespread-behavior/

https://www.theatlantic.com/technology/archive/2013/03/a-brief-history-of-applause-the-big-data-of-the-ancient-world/274014/
https://www.forbes.com/sites/kenmakovsky/2013/03/25/the-origins-of-applause/?sh=4d29ab831412
https://jborden.com/2021/02/17/heres-something-you-probably-never-wondered-about-the-history-of-clapping/#
https://www.npr.org/templates/story/story.php?storyId=199362737
https://www.psychologytoday.com/intl/blog/cutting-edge-leadership/202201/why-we-clap-the-psychology-applause
https://spsp.org/news/character-and-context-blog/crawley-clapping-facts-insights
https://www.todayifoundout.com/index.php/2016/04/people-first-start-clapping-show-appreciation-something/

Question 12: Why Is the Peace Sign Shaped the Way It Is?
https://www.britannica.com/story/where-did-the-peace-sign-come-from
https://coldwarstudies.com/2015/08/24/10-little-known-facts-about-the-peace-sign/#
https://en.wikipedia.org/wiki/Flag_semaphore
https://en.wikipedia.org/wiki/Peace_symbols
https://www.rd.com/article/history-of-peace-sign/
https://www.thoughtco.com/the-peace-symbol-1779351#

Question 13: Why are Four-Leaf Clovers Considered Lucky?
https://www.bhg.com/holidays/st-patricks-day/traditions/fun-facts-about-four-leaf-clovers/
https://www.countryliving.com/gardening/a42791437/four-leaf-clovers/
https://www.gardenweasel.com/groundbreakingtips/fun-facts-four-leaf-clovers/
https://kids.kiddle.co/Clover
https://parade.com/1327688/jessicasager/four-leaf-clover/
https://www.rd.com/article/four-leaf-clover/

Question 14: Why Do We Have Superstitions About Breaking Mirrors?
https://www.bbc.co.uk/programmes/articles/4jZWt1t6v0D-V33pLWD0KcT/on-reflection-eight-mysterious-facts-about-mirrors
https://en.wikipedia.org/wiki/Mirror
https://housecaravan.com/the-broken-mirror-symbolism/
https://kids.kiddle.co/Mirror

Part 2: The Human Body

Question 15: Why Do Most People Snore When Sleeping?
https://www.hopkinsmedicine.org/health/wellness-and-prevention/why-do-people-snore-answers-for-better-health
https://www.mayoclinic.org/diseases-conditions/snoring/symptoms-causes/syc-20377694
https://www.sleepadvisor.org/why-do-people-snore/
https://www.sleepfoundation.org/snoring/common-causes
https://veryhealthy.life/10-natural-solutions-to-stop-snoring/?msclkid=f62f17cd1c201f1f440772a1cbc73004

Question 16: Why Are Some People Left-Handed?
https://www.cnn.com/2015/11/03/health/being-left-handed-health-impact/index.html
https://elifesciences.org/articles/22784
https://www.factretriever.com/left-handedness-facts
https://www.insider.com/why-some-people-are-left-handed-2018-1ttps://www.livescience.com/what-causes-left-handedness.html
https://www.psychologytoday.com/us/blog/the-asymmetric-brain/202204/what-makes-someone-left-handed
https://www.rd.com/article/why-people-left-handed/
https://www.smithsonianmag.com/science-nature/why-are-some-people-left-handed-6556937/

Question 17: Why Do We Hiccup?
https://easyscienceforkids.com/hiccups/#google_vignette
https://www.healthline.com/health/how-to-get-rid-of-hiccups
https://www.thehealthy.com/digestive-health/hiccups-facts/
https://howtoadult.com/are-frequent-hiccups-anything-to-worry-about-in-children-8205969.html
https://www.playbuzz.com/jacobsmith11/14-fun-fact-about-hiccups
https://thrivemarket.com/blog/why-standing-on-your-head-wont-cure-hiccups-and-7-other-surprising-hiccups-facts

Question 18: Why Aren't Our Fingers the Same Length?
https://deserthandandpt.com/18-amazing-facts-about-human-hands/
https://www.eastwestcollege.com/fun-facts-about-the-human-hand/#
https://www.factsjustforkids.com/human-body-facts/hand-facts-for-kids/
www.handresearch.com/diagnostics/finger-length.htm
https://www.scienceabc.com/humans/why-arent-human-fingers-all-the-same-length.html
https://scifacts.net/human/length-of-fingers/
https://www.todayifoundout.com/index.php/2015/07/arent-fingers-length/

Question 19: Who Do We Have Almost No Hair Compared to Most Other Mammals?
https://www.almanac.com/fun-facts-and-myths-about-hair
https://www.bbc.com/future/article/20140926-are-hairy-faces-less-evolved
https://www.curlcentric.com/facts-about-hair/
https://phys.org/news/2023-01-today-tomorrow-humans-lost-body.html
https://www.scientificamerican.com/article/the-naked-truth-why-humans-have-no-fur/
https://www.simplyorganicbeauty.com/hair-facts/

Question 20: Why Do Our Fingertips and Toes Wrinkle If We Keep Them in Water a Long Time?
https://www.discovermagazine.com/the-sciences/why-do-fingers-get-wrinkly-after-a-long-bath-or-swim-a-biomedical-engineer
https://www.medicalnewstoday.com/articles/322705#conditions
https://www.newhealthadvisor.org/Functions-of-the-Skin.html
https://www.verywellhealth.com/why-do-fingers-wrinkle-2549395#

Question 21: Why Do Our Fingernails Grown Almost Twice as Fast as Our Toenails?
https://getlongnails.com/why-does-typing-stimulate-nail-growth/
https://www.healthline.com/health/beauty-skin-care/what-are-nails-made-of#16.-Cuticles-do-have-a-purpose
https://www.oregonlive.com/advice/2021/06/dear-doctor-what-does-fast-nail-growth-mean.html
https://www.scienceabc.com/humans/why-do-fingernails-grow-faster-than-toenails.html#
https://vitaclix.com/why-do-we-have-nails/

Question 22: Why Are Our Lips Pink?
https://amazingfacts4u.com/lip/
https://www.bbc.com/future/article/20150112-why-do-we-have-lips
https://www.boldsky.com/insync/pulse/2017/interesting-facts-about-lips/articlecontent-pf147922-111064.html
https://www.cbsnews.com/news/the-science-behind-puckering-up/
https://www.everydaycares.com/lips/lip-color-and-health/
https://www.healthline.com/health/different-lip-types-and-how-to-take-care-of-them

https://www.healthline.com/health/how-to-make-lips-pink
https://www.medicalnewstoday.com/articles/how-to-get-pink-lips-naturally
https://www.positivemed.com/2016/08/02/lip-colors/

Question 23: Why Do Most Teenagers Get Pimples?
https://www.goodhousekeeping.com/beauty/anti-aging/tips/a25082/acne-facts/
https://www.mayoclinic.org/diseases-conditions/acne/symptoms-causes/syc-20368047
https://www.medicalnewstoday.com/articles/315104#treatments
https://www.msn.com/en-us/health/symptoms/Pus/hp-pus
https://www.insider.com/what-is-inside-your-pimples-acne-2017-8
https://skincaregeeks.com/popped-a-pimple-and-something-hard-came-out/
https://www.webmd.com/skin-problems-and-treatments/what-to-know-about-milia
https://www.wederm.com/2015/05/28/weird-facts-about-acne/

Part 3: Nature – Plants, Animals and Weather

Question 24: Why Do Rabbits Wiggle Their Noses?
https://bunnyasapet.com/why-do-rabbits-wiggle-their-nose/
https://lionheadrabbitcare.com/rabbit-nose-facts/
https://www.livescience.com/60752-human-senses.html
https://www.onlinerabbitcare.com/questions-and-answers/why-do-rabbits-wiggle-their-noses/
https://petkeen.com/why-do-rabbits-noses-twitch-and-wiggle/
https://www.quantamagazine.org/how-a-human-smell-receptor-works-is-finally-revealed-20230501/

Question 25: Why Do Fish Live in Schools?
https://www.aqueon.com/articles/schooling-fish
https://www.letshealthify.com/why-do-some-fish-travel-in-schools/
https://www.sciencefocus.com/nature/how-do-schools-of-fish-swim-in-perfect-unison
https://www.thesprucepets.com/schooling-fish-1378344
https://travelprojection.com/why-do-fish-travel-in-schools/

Question 26: Why Are Flies Attracted to Poop?
https://a-z-animals.com/blog/do-flies-poop/
https://www.atshq.org/why-do-flies-like-poop/
https://kidadl.com/facts/why-do-flies-like-poop-here-are-the-disgusting-reasons
https://www.thelist.com/258435/why-are-flies-attracted-to-poop/
https://www.orkin.com/pests/flies/house-flies/gestation-of-a-house-fly
https://wheeliebincleaningservice.com/do-flies-lay-eggs-or-maggots/
https://yardandgardenguru.com/why-are-flies-attracted-to-poop/

Question 27: Why Do Cows Have Nose Rings?
https://farmandchill.com/why-do-cows-have-nose-rings/
https://kb.rspca.org.au/knowledge-base/what-are-the-animal-welfare-issues-with-weaning-nose-rings-and-other-anti-suckling-devices-for-calves/
https://piercinghome.com/what-does-a-nose-ring-mean-on-a-woman/
https://quickanimals.com/cows-rings-nose/
https://www.scienceabc.com/nature/animals/why-do-some-bulls-have-nose-rings.html
https://untamedanimals.com/why-do-bulls-and-cows-have-a-nose-ring/
https://yardandgardenguru.com/why-do-cows-have-nose-rings/
https://www.thespruce.com/irish-shamrocks-and-4-leaf-clovers-2130966

Question 28: Why Do Dogs Turn Around and Around Before Lying Down?
https://www.emotionalpetsupport.com/2020/09/how-do-dogs-
https://en.wikipedia.org/wiki/Domesticationsleep/
https://www.nationalgeographic.com/animals/article/domesticated-animals
https://www.silentnight.ae/blogs/your-guide-to-better-sleep/fascinating-sleep-facts-about-dogsx
https://www.thesprucepets.com/why-do-dogs-circle-before-they-lay-down-5120874
https://us.dogfriendlyco.com/blogs/articles/5-facts-about-dog-sleep
https://vcahospitals.com/know-your-pet/why-dogs-turn-around-before-lying-down
https://wagenabled.com/4-facts-about-dogs-sleep-habits/
https://yumove.co.uk/blogs/health-guides/10-facts-about-sleeping-dogs

Question 29: Why Do Cats Rub Against People's Legs?
https://a-z-animals.com/blog/the-6-reasons-cats-rub-against-you-and-if-should-you-let-them/
https://www.catmastermind.com/why-does-cats-rub-against-your- ttps://ikittycat.com/why-do-cats-rub-against-you-then-bite/legs/ttps://www.petmd.com/cat/behavior/why-do-cats-rub-against-you
https://en.wikipedia.org/wiki/Cat_intelligence
https://www.factretriever.com/cat-facts
https://petkeen.com/cat-facts/
https://www.petsradar.com/advice/why-do-cats-rub-against-you
https://www.rover.com/blog/why-do-cats-rub-against-you/
https://www.thesprucepets.com/why-cats-rub-against-legs-5210427
https://welovecatsandkittens.com/cat-info/cat-facts/
https://www.worthycat.com/the-shocking-truth-about-why-do-cats-rub-on-you/

Question 30: Why Do Cats Sit on Mounds of Clothes?
https://en.wikipedia.org/wiki/Cat_intelligence
https://www.factretriever.com/cat-facts
https://www.konnecthq.com/cat-facts/#google_vignette
https://www.msn.com/en-us/lifestyle/lifestyle-buzz/why-does-your-cat-sit-on-your-clothes-12-reasons-why
https://welovecatsandkittens.com/cat-info/cat-facts/

Question 31: Why Is There Snow on Mountaintops if Heat Rises?
www.primaryhomeworkhelp.co.uk/mountains/climate.htm#
https://www.sciencefocus.com/planet-earth/why-is-it-colder-at-the-top-of-a-mountain-if-youre-closer-to-the-sun
https://wisdomanswer.com/why-do-most-mountains-in-warm-climates-have-snow-on-the-top/
https://www.wonderopolis.org/wonder/do-all-mountains-wear-snowcaps

Question 32: Why Do We Have Different Time Zones Around the World?
https://fi.edu/en/blog/who-created-time-zones
https://geojango.com/blogs/explore-your-world/history-of-time-zones
https://www.history.com/this-day-in-history/galileo-is-accused-of-heresy
https://www.infoplease.com/calendars/history/time-zone-origins
https://www.sciencekids.co.nz/sciencefacts/time.html#google_vignette
https://www.thoughtco.com/what-are-time-zones-1435358
https://www.thoughtco.com/why-we-have-time-zones-1773953
https://www.timeanddate.com/time/current-number-time-zones.html
https://www.timeanddate.com/fun/time-date-trivia.html

https://www.timeanddate.com/time/zone/uk
https://veryinformed.com/why-are-there-different-time-zones/

Question 33: Why Do Leaves Change Colors in Autumn?
https://allthatsinteresting.com/why-leaves-change-color#Why%20Leaves%20Change%20Color
https://askabiologist.asu.edu/questions/why-do-leaves-change-color
https://www.fs.usda.gov/visit/fall-colors/science-of-fall-colors
https://www.rutgers.edu/news/why-do-leaves-change-color
https://www.si.edu/stories/why-do-leaves-change-color-fall

Question 34: Why Are Some Stars Brighter Than Other Stars?
https://cosmicopia.gsfc.nasa.gov/qa_star.html
https://en.wikipedia.org/wiki/List_of_nearest_stars_and_brown_dwarfs
https://en.wikipedia.org/wiki/Star_Light,_Star_Bright
https://www.juniorsbook.com/tell-me-why/why-are-some-stars-brighter-than-others/
https://phys.libretexts.org/Bookshelves/Astronomy__Cosmology/Astronomy_1e_%28OpenStax%29/17%3A_Analyzing_Starlight/17.01%3A_The_Brightness_of_Stars
https://pirateering.com/why-are-some-stars-brighter-than-others/
https://starregister.org/some-stars-brighter-than-others.php

Question 35: Why Do We Wish on Stars?
https://dailyjag.com/offbeat/why-do-people-make-a-wish-when-they-see-a-falling-star/
https://en.wikipedia.org/wiki/Star_Light,_Star_Bright
https://exemplore.com/magic/Do-Shooting-Stars-Have-the-Power-to-Fulfill-Wishes
https://mcnicholasmilestone.com/2011/12/09/why-you-wish-upon-a-star-the-stories-behind-the-superstitions/
https://medium.com/illumination/should-i-make-a-wish-on-shooting-stars-8284c068388e
https://science.howstuffworks.com/dictionary/astronomy-terms/leonid.htm
https://www.thesimplethings.com/blog/stories-behind-superstitions-wishing-on-star
https://space-facts.com/stars/
https://symbolsage.com/symbolism-of-shooting-stars/

Part 4: Business And Community

Question 36: Why Do Medical Doctors Wear White Lab Coats?
ttps://www.ama-assn.org/medical-students/medical-school-life/meaning-behind-your-white-coat
ttps://www.aamc.org/news/white-coat-symbol-professionalism-or-hierarchical-elitism
ttps://en.wikipedia.org/wiki/White_coat
ttps://intivahealth.com/blog/why-a-doctor-wears-a-white-coat/
ttps://journalofethics.ama-assn.org/article/doctors-white-coat-historical-perspective/2007-04
ttps://www.mentalfloss.com/article/637686/why-hospital-doctors-wear-white-coats

Question 37: Why Do Many Police Cars Have a Red Light Above the Police Officer Driving and a Blue Light Above the Officer's Partner?
https://en.wikipedia.org/wiki/Emergency_vehicle_lighting
https://www.jeffhurtblog.com/the-real-reason-behind-vehicle-emergency-lights-being-red-and-blue/
https://www.ukemergency.co.uk/blue-light-use/

Question 38: Why Do Many Churches Have Steeples?
https://aleteia.org/2017/08/02/this-is-why-churches-have-steeples/
https://www.caniry.com/whats-the-difference-between-a-spire-and-steeple/

https://edenbengals.com/what-does-the-steeple-of-a-church-symbolize/
https://en.wikipedia.org/wiki/Old_North_Church
https://en.wikipedia.org/wiki/Steeple
https://en.wikipedia.org/wiki/Ulm_Minster
https://en.wikipedia.org/wiki/Whitewash
https://www.engineeringcivil.com/what-is-white-washing-and-why-is-it-done.html
https://livingpraying.com/why-do-churches-have-steeples/
https://www.patheos.com/blogs/christiancrier/2015/09/21/why-do-churches-have-steeples-where-did-this-tradition-begin/
https://www.timesmojo.com/why-do-churches-have-steeples-on-them/

Question 39: Why Do Railroad Tracks Often Have Gravel Under Them?
https://en.wikipedia.org/wiki/Track_ballast
https://en.wikipedia.org/wiki/Ballastless_track
https://www.mentalfloss.com/article/85234/why-are-there-crushed-stones-alongside-railroad-tracks
https://www.scienceabc.com/pure-sciences/why-are-there-stones-train-ballast-alongside-railway-tracks.html
https://www.survivaltechshop.com/train-weight/
https://tenrandomfacts.com/railroad-track/
https://www.yyrail.com/latest-news/gravel-on-the-railway-tracks-what-are-they-used-for.html

Question 40: Why Are Bedrooms Typically on the Second Floor of a Two-Story House?
https://blog.ansi.org/why-do-we-sleep-upstairs/
com/blogs/news/benefits-of-a-two-story-home
https://en.wikipedia.org/wiki/Knocker-up
greenbuildingforum.co.uk/newforum/comments.php?DiscussionID=9114ttps://saterdesign.
https://www.randkcustomhomes.net/upstairs-downstairs-master-bedroom-pros-cons/

Part 5: Traditions in Western Society

Question 41: Why Do We Shout, "Happy New Year" and Blow Noisemakers When the New Year Begins?
https://en.wikipedia.org/wiki/History_of_calendars#
https://en.wikipedia.org/wiki/New_Year
https://gluesticksgumdrops.com/easy-noisemakers-new-years-eve/#
https://www.grunge.com/681618/the-real-reason-we-make-so-much-noise-at-midnight-on-new-years-eve/
https://medium.com/@michrkarr/why-southerners-eat-black-eyed-peas-and-greens-for-luck-on-new-years-day-22cc618f5213
https://www.pumpitupparty.com/blog/how-did-the-tradition-of-birthdays-begin/
https://projectnursery.com/2013/12/new-years-eve-noisemakers/
https://www.southernliving.com/holidays-occasions/new-years/noise-on-new-years-eve#

Question 42: Why Shouldn't You Wear White After Labor Day?
https://www.ducksters.com/holidays/labor_day.php
https://emilypost.com/advice/wearing-white-after-labor-day
https://en.wikipedia.org/wiki/Bank_holiday
https://www.farmersalmanac.com/wear-white-after-labor-day-35950
https://learningenglish.voanews.com/a/why-americans-don-t-wear-white-after-labor-day/5060464.html
https://www.newsweek.com/no-white-after-labor-day-fact-fiction-experts-1739445
https://www.southernliving.com/holidays-occasions/labor-day/why-cant-you-wear-white-after-labor-day
https://www.newsweek.com/wear-white-after-labor-day-explained-1625860

https://www.thepioneerwoman.com/holidays-celebrations/a40246129/white-after-labor-day-history/
https://www.the-sun.com/news/3569204/why-cant-you-wear-white-after-labor-day/
https://www.usatoday.com/story/life/2022/08/12/white-after-labor-day-explained/10269739002/

Question 43: Why Do We Go Door-To-Door Collecting Candy on Halloween?
https://www.businessinsider.com/trick-or-treating-halloween-history-2019-10
https://en.wikipedia.org/wiki/Trick-or-treating
https://www.history.com/news/halloween-trick-or-treating-origins
https://www.nationalgeographic.com/culture/article/the-history-of-trick-or-treating-and-how-it-became-a-halloween-tradition
https://people.howstuffworks.com/culture-traditions/holidays-halloween/why-we-trick-or-treat.htm

Question 44: Why is the Day After America's Thanksgiving Festival Called Black Friday?
https://www.aol.com/lifestyle/black-friday-origin-why-called-031211451.html
https://www.augustman.com/sg/news/black-friday-history-and-meaning/
https://www.britannica.com/story/why-is-it-called-black-friday
https://www.businessinsider.com/guides/deals/why-is-it-called-black-Friday
https://www.snopes.com/fact-check/black-friday-origins/
https://www.usatoday.com/story/money/shopping/2023/11/13/why-is-it-called-black-friday/71505973007/
https://wwd.com/feature/why-is-it-called-black-friday-history-1235941382/

Question 45: Why Do We Americans Sing the National Anthem at Sporting Events?
https://www.americanhistoryforkids.com/star-spangled-banner/
https://en.wikipedia.org/wiki/The_Star-Spangled_Banner
https://www.history.com/this-day-in-history/key-pens-star-spangled-banner
https://www.history.com/topics/19th-century/the-star-spangled-banner
https://www.ibtimes.com/national-anthem-day-interesting-facts-about-star-spangled-banner-3422003
https://kids.kiddle.co/The_Star-Spangled_Banner
https://medium.com/@ellesmythy/the-invented-tradition-of-standing-for-the-national-anthem-603f2d33a295
https://www.si.edu/spotlight/flag-day/banner-facts
https://starspangledflags.com/6-fun-facts-about-the-star-spangled-banner/
https://time.com/4955623/history-national-anthem-sports-nfl/
https://time.com/5289276/national-anthem-standing-rule-history/

Question 46: Why Do Men Get on Bended Knee to Propose Marriage?
https://www.abc10.com/article/entertainment/television/programs/why-guy-question/proposals-one-knee-marriage-engagement/
https://www.brides.com/story/propose-on-one-knee-tradition
https://mennstuff.com/why-do-men-kneel-to-propose/#Which_Knee_Does_A_Man_Kneel_On_When_Proposing
https://www.mentalfloss.com/article/640187/why-do-people-get-down-one-knee-marriage-proposals
https://www.southwestoriginals.com/heres-why-men-get-down-on-one-knee-to-propose/

Question 47: Why Do We Turn Our Clocks Ahead in the Spring and Turn Them Back in the Fall?
https://www.bbc.co.uk/bitesize/articles/z6kdpg8
https://en.wikipedia.org/wiki/Daylight_saving_time_by_country
https://www.history.com/news/why-do-we-have-daylight-saving-time
https://www.webexhibits.org/daylightsaving/b.html
https://news.yahoo.com/daylight-saving-time-fall-back

Question 48: Why Do We Say "Cheese" as a Picture Is Being Taken?
https://www.mamalisa.com/blog/say-cheese-whats-said-around-the-world-when-a-photo-is-taken/
https://www.scienceandmediamuseum.org.uk/objects-and-stories/first-digital-photos#
https://www.swedishnomad.com/facts-about-cheese/
https://www.todayifoundout.com/index.php/2013/04/the-origin-of-say-cheese-and-when-people-started-smiling-in-photographs/

Question 49: Why Do Many People Believe Thirteen is an Unlucky Number?
https://theconversation.com/why-is-13-considered-unlucky-explaining-the-power-of-its-bad-reputation-191477
ttps://en.wikipedia.org/wiki/Say_cheese
https://en.wikipedia.org/wiki/13_(number)
https://www.history.com/news/whats-so-unlucky-about-the-number-13
https://www.msn.com/en-us/news/other/13-fascinating-facts-about-friday-the-13th

Question 50: Why Do Children Hide Teeth Under Their Pillow for the Tooth Fairy?
https://en.wikipedia.org/wiki/Tooth_fairy
https://www.healthline.com/health/childrens-health/baby-teeth-fall-out
https://www.mayoclinic.org/healthy-lifestyle/childrens-health/expert-answers/baby-teeth/faq-20058532
https://www.123dentist.com/a-brief-history-of-the-tooth-fairy/
https://toothshow.com/what-is-the-name-of-the-tooth-fairy/

BACK COVER

Most people look at the world and just assume that things are the way they are just because they are. When one looks closer, though, it becomes clear that this world is a weird place. No matter what one thinks about - other countries, our bodies, animals, our planet, and our own society – there are strange happenings that raise the question of why:

Why does the United Kingdom celebrate Boxing Day?

Why do Germans celebrate Oktoberfest?

Why are our fingers different lengths?

Why do people snore?

Why are some stars brighter than others?

Why do doctors wear white coats?

Why do children hide their teeth for the Tooth Fairy?

These and numerous other questions are answered in this book. Not only will you learn the answer to 50 "why" questions, you will also learn how to ask a good "why" question. Although learning the answers to the fifty questions may appeal to you most now, being able to ask and answer questions is a lifelong skill. This book will allow you to amaze your friends, serve as a reference, and assist in preparing you for life.

LONG BLURB

The world is a strange place when you stop and think about it – here's why!

＋＋＋＋＋＋＋＋＋＋＋＋＋＋＋＋＋＋＋＋＋＋＋＋＋＋＋＋＋＋＋

SHORT BLURB

When "just because" isn't enough – it's good to know why.

www.ingramcontent.com/pod-product-compliance
Lightning Source LLC
Chambersburg PA
CBHW071006120626
46546CB00003B/949